SIGNED

IRONWILL FOOTBALL'S RECRUITING GUIDE FOR CANADIAN HIGH SCHOOL FOOTBALL PLAYERS

COACH TIM BURRIS

IRON WILL
FOOTBALL

tellwell

Tellwell Talent
www.tellwell.ca

ISBN
978-0-2288-8213-8 (Hardcover)
978-0-2288-8212-1 (Paperback)
978-0-2288-8214-5 (eBook)

DEDICATION

To my world, Red and Blaise. Thank you for the endless support and encouragement.

Thank you to my good friend and former Canadian Football League player Paul Archer for your contributions to this book.

TABLE OF CONTENTS

ACKNOWLEDGMENTS

I would like to thank the coaches, players, and parents who contributed to and helped support this book by taking the time to provide feedback and share their personal experiences. Without your help and passion for assisting the development of football, this book would not have been possible.

PREFACE

To be honest, I should have written this book years ago, after my football career ended in 2007. I grew up in Scarborough, Ontario, and I have had the honour of playing with and against some of the most talented football players in Canada. Looking back to when I played high school football, I realized that not all of the talented football players made it playing football past high school, and this is still the current trend. When talking to players I coached and their parents, the insight that continues to come up is there is a lack of support and guidance student athletes receive when navigating the next steps to play football at the post-secondary level, and this really gets my blood heated.

I believe that, regardless of their talent level, every Canadian high school football player and their family must know what options and opportunities are available after high school, and how the recruiting process works. Football recruiting shouldn't be a secret. The recruiting information should be crystal clear so educated decisions about pursuing football at the next level can be made. It is far too common that high school football players are making last-resort decisions about where they will play football after high school because recruiting information is limited or inaccessible, or players are finding out too late when to start the recruiting process.

There is nothing worse than having an end goal in mind, but an unclear pathway. As you go through the football recruiting process, you will make over a hundred decisions as you choose your post-secondary football program. The transition from high school to the next stage of life is one of the most challenging moves you will make in your career.

When you are deciding what university, junior, or CEGEP[1] football program to commit to, you have to realize that your decision will be based on more than just football. You must think about where you want to be twenty years from now, and consider the dedication required to execute that plan. Once you have that long-term vision, you need to be confident about your commitment.

If you are a football player and are taking the time to read this book, you are most likely interested in learning about the recruiting process and what football options are available after high school. If you're a parent, you are probably looking for ways to help your child achieve their dream of playing football at the post-secondary level.

The purpose of this book is to help inform and guide you through the recruiting process to avoid the pitfalls of confusion and self-doubt, which can result in failure. In Canada, there is a lack of awareness and accessible information about football recruiting, post-secondary football options, and clear pathways to university, college, or junior football. The contributing factors depend on who the high school coach is. If a high school or community coach in Canada has not played football past high school, it will be hard for them to help their players, as their recruiting insight will be limited. Secondly, if these coaches are not known to coaches at the university or junior levels, it can be a challenge to establish connections to help their players, which results in their player trying to get recruited on their own, without guidance.

This book is a vital tool for discovering your pathway and learning how and when to start your recruiting journey. It includes important recruiting and academic details, plans for campus visits, examples of introduction letters and football résumés for post-secondary coaches, and action-plan checklists that give you the blueprint for achieving your goals. The action-plan checklists give you detailed outlines on the steps you need to take from Grades 9 through 12 to ensure a smooth recruiting process. The transition from high school football will be a lot

---

[1] *Collège d'enseignement général et professionnel*

smoother with an understanding of the recruiting process, awareness of the steps required to generate exposure, and details on how to start the recruiting journey. This book covers common questions players and parents have asked us at the IRONWILL Football Performance Camps. There is a chapter included specifically for parents, in which we dive into questions that parents have asked us about football development, recruiting, and options after high school, and common pitfalls that lead to recruiting failure.

I wish I'd had this information to help guide me when I was playing football. It would have saved my family and me a lot of time, money, and frustration. This is the motivation behind the writing of this book—to save you from having to go through what I did.

BEFORE WE GET STARTED

I want to be very clear with players and families from the beginning: student athletes who are proactive during the recruiting process will find success. Their responsibilities are to their studies first, followed by athletics. It is unrealistic to follow the steps in this book but ignore academics, strength and conditioning training, or positional training and expect to see positive results. If you want to succeed, you can't expect to simply train on the field while ignoring your studies.

It is unrealistic to expect an Athletic Financial Award (Canada) or a Division 1 full scholarship (USA) if you are not:

- one of the top players in the country
- training and aspiring to be the best
- academically focused

If you are a player, you will not reach your goals without being responsible to your studies. A positive performance on game day, solid grades, and good character will attract coaches throughout the country, and help you transition to the next level after high school.

This book is for high school players who are committed to moving on to playing football at the university level or at the junior level, and finding out how to go about reaching their football goals. Recruiting is competitive between teams at the university and junior levels; the only way teams win games and championships is by bringing on the best players. As a student athlete, you are competing against other players during the recruiting process, in the classroom, and on the football field.

You will attract more interest from post-secondary football programs when you make plays for your team and perform at an elite level during games and in school. There is no other way around it: you can't expect Canadian university coaches to provide financial awards to players who do not make the dress roster on game day, or who cannot maintain a respectable grade-point average. Remember this: performance is everything.

ALLOW ME TO INTRODUCE MYSELF

I always knew I had the talent and skills to play at the university level. To be honest, I was a *dawg* on the football field—I played and dominated like a giant. The biggest strike against me was that I was an undersized defensive lineman, so coaches at the university level were always on the fence about recruiting me. A quick story: Coming off a standout fall football season playing in the CEGEP league in Quebec, I was ready to showcase my talents at the high school recruiting evaluation combine I attended in Montreal, Quebec. My group was with the defensive linemen, and we completed a wide range of drills that evaluated our athletic ability. I tested very well in all of them. Then we moved on to defensive vs. offensive line one-on-one pass-rush drills. I knew that I was too skilled athletically to simply perform a pass-rush finesse move to win, so I decided to use a power move to show off another part of my skill set. I did a bull rush move and put the offensive lineman on his back, right in front of the University of Akron scout and multiple NCAA and Canadian university coaches. I thought I was going to get receive a Division 1 scholarship offer on the spot after my solid performance. After the combine, the Akron scout came up to my coach and me and said, "I want to make you an offer right now, but I can't sign a 5'10" defensive linemen because I would lose my job." I will never forget those words. They were a dagger to the heart.

A little bit of self-doubt crept into my mind. If I was so good, how come coaches were not knocking on my door to recruit me?

Having this slow start forced me to be proactive and take recruiting into my own hands. I just didn't know where to start. How would I contact recruiters and coaches? What grades did I need to get into school? When were the admission applications due, who (and when) did I send my highlight and game film to, what do I say when I finally talk to coaches? These were just a few obstacles I overcame during my recruiting process. I struggled with anxiety because I didn't want to waste my talent and not reach my goal. But I knew I had to fight to make my dream come true.

After overcoming multiple obstacles, I finally signed to a U Sports team, St. Mary's University in Halifax, Nova Scotia, where I was a freshmen starter on the St. Mary's Huskies national champion team. And most importantly, I graduated!

My name is Coach Tim Burris, and I am known as Coach B in the Alberta football community and across Canada. For the past ten years, my mission has been to help young Canadian football players develop their skills. I educate players on what it takes to play football after high school, and provide them with a blueprint to achieving post-secondary-level recruitment and beyond.

I am the owner-operator of IRONWILL Football Performance Camps. We develop players' football skills, and provide them with football development and recruiting insight to generate exposure to post-secondary football opportunities across Canada. Our mandate at IRONWILL Football is to offer the highest-level performance camps and position-specific programs for players to develop their skills and achieve their goals. This book's purpose is to compel a higher standard of recruits, pushing the bar to new heights for Canadian football development.

If you've seen me working with players, you'll already know that I am passionate about guiding student athletes along the steps they need to take to play football at the next level after high school. This is my dream, and I am thankful for the opportunity to share my insight and experiences with you.

As a football coach, the bottom line is that I want to see you win, achieve your football goals, and be successful. As you read this book, you might feel a bit overwhelmed by all the information provided. But by the end of the book I guarantee that you will have a better understanding of how the recruiting process works, and you will be able to make educated decisions on your future as a student athlete. I will show you how, so let's get ready to win!

If you need additional help or are interested in attending any of our performance camps or programs, visit www.ironwillfootball.ca to get in touch. Also, feel free to contact me at coachburris@ironwillfootball.ca if you still have questions I can assist with.

Not every player is going to be All Canadian or have every university knocking at their door, and that's okay. It doesn't mean you're not a great player. However, we will teach you the options that are available to you to play football after high school and what you need to achieve your goals. Players need to understand that they cannot wait for coaches to come knocking, especially in Canada. Recruiting budgets aren't large enough, and the manpower required isn't available to travel multiple times across the country to recruit players.

I present you this book, which contains insight developed through my own recruiting experiences, helping other players reach their football recruiting goals, and coaching at every level from bantam to university football.

Congratulations on taking your first steps toward your pursuit of playing post-secondary football. I want you to have a smooth recruiting process and a successful transition to playing football at the next level. I don't want you to miss out. All the processes and steps are laid out for you in this book, so just follow along.

CHAPTER 1

Setting the Tone

Some players transition smoothly into post-secondary football. Others do not. Why? We begin by asking, "What skills or characteristics do the successful players possess that others do not?"

Please check the boxes that apply to you:

Successful football players:	
Understand the recruiting process and the multiple post-secondary football pathways	☐
Are mature and understand time management	☐
Have a strong support system, including family, coaches, and academic faculty	☐
Have patience and a strong work ethic	☐
Have a vision and set clear goals to achieve	☐
Are academically successful and love to learn	☐
Have a positive attitude	☐
Are not interested in instant gratification	☐
Understand what they need to do to get to the next level	☐
Take action to achieve goals, complete tasks, and execute at the right time	☐
Focus on the key areas that will help them get to the next level	☐

Do you possess these skills and characteristics? If there are skills and characteristics you don't have, write a list below and include notes on how to develop each of these skills.

I call the player who had all the talent on the football field and academic grades but failed to transition to the post-secondary level the "hometown hero." These types of players will always be remembered as great local athletes who never made it past high school. I don't want you to be just a hometown hero. Below are some obstacles that might block your path.

Please check the boxes that apply to you:

The football players who are not successful in transitioning to the next level often:	
Are not provided with enough information about how to get to the next level	☐
Lack mentorship, guidance, and parent involvement	☐
Procrastinate and fear the unknown	☐
Wait for coaches to recruit them	☐
Are not willing to put in the time to improve their football skills	☐
Lack maturity	☐
Have a large ego and are unwilling to learn	☐
Have no plan outside of football	☐
Possess poor time management	☐
Set unrealistic expectations	☐
Lack passion for the process	☐
Are afraid to ask for help if they're struggling academically or in life	☐

Does any of the above sound like you? Grab a pen right now and write down what you can do now to change to be successful.

HOW TO START

A successful transition plan starts with deciding and committing to football at the post-secondary level and then developing a plan around where you want to play. Take this seriously. You need a plan to have a smooth transition to the post-secondary level. Believe me when I say this: You need to be honest with yourself and determine which pathway best suits you.

In Canada, there is one high school route and three post-secondary pathways a student athlete can take:

1. University football (U Sports), or the National Collegiate Athletic Association (NCAA)
2. Junior football
3. CEGEP football
4. High school prep school

Alternatively, student athletes can participate in a combination of junior or CEGEP football, then move on to the university level.

If you have the desire to play in the NCAA in the States, make sure to read the Canadian high school prep school section on page 11 and the chapter on NCAA football page 24. These will help you get started with the process.

When I say to be honest with yourself, I mean you need to ask some key questions. This also means *knowing* yourself and understanding your personal weaknesses, strengths, and skill sets. When you honestly answer the questions below, you will figure out which direction you should head after high school.

Knowing yourself is the most important part of your journey. When you really take the time examine your motivation, the direction you need to follow will be clear.

COACH BURRIS INSIGHT:

I would suggest sitting down with your parent or guardian when you answer the following three questionnaires. They will help provide perspective and keep you honest. Trust those who know you best!

Answer the following questions if you want to be a student athlete at the *university level*:

Would you be attending university if you didn't play football? Why or why not?

Do you enjoy academics and learning, and attending lectures and labs? Why or why not?

Do you have good study habits? How are your note-taking skills?

How are your organizational and time-management skills?

University academics is an independent learning model. Do you always need someone to remind you to complete readings and assignments? Why or why not?

Do you have the grade point average (GPA) necessary to be accepted into university?

Do you know what GPA you need to be accepted into university?

What would you like to major in at university?

Do you have the financial resources to go to post-secondary school?

Can you handle the pressure to constantly compete in the film room, at practice, and on game day? Why or why not?

Do you feel comfortable living away from home? Why or why not?

Answer the following questions if you want to follow the *junior football* route:

Would you rather pursue a trade or other work and still play football at a high level instead of going to university? Why or why not?
Are you unsure if you want to attend university? Why or why not?
Do you need to upgrade your academics to be accepted into university?
Would an additional year or two of football development help you reach your goal of playing football at the university level? Why or why not?

Do you want to work and play football at a higher level after graduating high school? Why or why not?
Do you enjoy competition? Why or why not?

Answer the following questions if you want to go the *CEGEP* route:

Are you comfortable living away from home? Why or why not?
Is academic upgrading and football development something that you need?

Could you benefit from receiving support to decide which direction to take your student athlete career? Why or why not?
Do you need more football film to send to coaches?
Do you thrive in a highly competitive football environment? Why or why not?

Answer the following questions if you want to follow the *high school prep* route:

Is your goal to play at the NCAA or U Sports level? Why or why not?

Do you want to earn your high school academic diploma and receive support and guidance in order to be accepted into university in Canada or in the United States? Why or why not?
Are you looking to gain more exposure by playing an American high school schedule?
Are you interested in playing one or two years of American high school football to develop your game?
Do you need direction on what post-secondary opportunities are available to you as a student athlete?
Do you want to be a part of a program that focuses on academics and football development? Why or why not?

CANADIAN PREP HIGH SCHOOL

Another option that is becoming popular for high school players is attending a Canadian prep high school. You might be asking yourself, "What is a prep school?" Well, it's a high school football program that focuses on preparing student athletes academically and athletically to play at the NCAA or U Sports level. In addition, prep high school helps the student athlete prepare to write the SAT, and to achieve the academic entrance requirements to attend an NCAA and/or U Sports program.

The reason Canadian players are starting to play at prep high schools is that games are played against American high schools. This provides a lot of exposure opportunities and the chance to play at a higher level of high school competition.

> *High school prep schools play good competition and that's what the US college coaches look for when it comes to Canadian kids. They don't know if they can play American ball. So that gives them a platform, for real.*
>
> Justin Sambu
> University of Maine
> Canadian Prep School Alumni

WHAT YOU NEED TO KNOW

- There are fees involved in attending Canadian prep high school.
- If you will live out of your home province, you will need to find room and board unless the school has arrangements.
- You will require a passport to travel to the United States.

BENEFITS OF A CANADIAN PREP HIGH SCHOOL

The following are potential benefits of prep high school, depending on what type of high school football experience you want:

1. Academic learning in a small-class setting
2. The opportunity to play against American high school teams
3. Increased exposure, because games are played in the United States against American high school football teams
4. The opportunity to gain experience playing American rules football
5. Opportunities for NCAA scholarships or U Sports offers

COACH BURRIS INSIGHT:

This book does not endorse any high school or post-secondary football program, but our aim is to inform you of all available options. Please do your research on any football program of interest.

Keep in mind that it's not a guarantee that student athletes will receive an NCAA scholarship or a U Sports offer by playing at a prep school. Your game-day performance and academics will dictate what interest you generate at the post-secondary level.

CHAPTER 2

Football Options After High School Graduation

You have taken the first of many steps needed to put yourself in the best possible position to succeed in post-secondary education and football by completing the previous chapter. The ideal time to start considering your football future is around Grade 9, but don't worry if you're getting started later than that, as we can still guide you through the process, but understand that you will need to put in a lot more work in a much shorter amount of time.

Let's dive into your football options after high school graduation.

CANADIAN UNIVERSITY FOOTBALL

The highest level of amateur football is played at the university level. Student athletes who enjoy academics and know the professional career path they would like to pursue find the most success in university. Playing university football is highly competitive, and there are standards each player must meet. Before you get excited, know that playing university football in Canada is a pay-to-play model: costs include athletic fees to play while you attend school. Your main objectives as a university student athlete are to maximize your academic potential and your athletic talents, and graduate with minimal debt.

High school players who perform at an exceptional level on game day throughout their high school careers will generate interest from university football programs. Most importantly, your academic grades are your lifeline to playing football at the university level. A student athlete's academic performance will ultimately determine which football program he can take advantage of after high school.

To be crystal clear with you, there is *no way* you can play university football if you do not meet the academic standards that university admissions require. University coaches will only take student athletes seriously when they know they excel academically. Have your academic transcripts prepared when the university comes calling.

> *There are a few things, looking back at my experience, that I think are important for young guys to consider. Research the school, and make sure it offers the program you want. I would encourage young guys to make sure they take advantage of the opportunity to have football assist with their education from a financial standpoint. Secondly, make sure it's a good fit. You're going to spend the next four to six years at the university, so you want to make sure you consider all your options before committing to a program. Lastly, get in the weight room . . . it's such a big transition from high school to university, and having a good starting point from a strength perspective will help that transition.*

Tyler Ledwos
IRONWILL Football alumni; University of Calgary Alumni; University of Calgary Dinos receiver

If you want to play U Sports, the following steps will help you:

1. Make a list of the universities you would like to attend as a student athlete (refer to Chapter 6: Making a Recruiting List for more details).
2. Research the academic programs and grades required to be accepted into your program of interest.
3. Research the football program. Things to look for during your research:
   - The roster and the depth charts to see how many players are in your position

- The players on the roster who play your position, and see how many more years of eligibility they have left
- Research new recruits who will be signed on and note if any will be playing your position

COACH BURRIS INSIGHT:

The position depth chart will help you gain player personnel insight. For example, you may not want to attend a school with ten players ahead of you who play the same position, as you may not see the field for a couple of years.

4. Measurables: When reviewing the roster, look at the height and weight of players in your position to see if you are in the same range of body type. Canadian universities are less strict with players' measurables compared to the NCCA Division 1 schools. However, it is still a good idea to see where you are in comparison to other players in your position at the U Sports level. (See "Players' Body Type" in Chapter 3.)
5. Read up on the head coaches' bios to understand their coaching background and philosophy. Make sure to look up the head coach, position coach, and recruiting coordinator information. Also look at their previous season's record and national football ranking. You can find the information on team websites.
6. Once you've completed your research, rank the top 10 Canadian universities you would like to attend.
7. Start to make contact with the football programs. Send in your football résumé, film, academic grades, and program of interest. If the university football program is impressed by your grades and application, they may invite you for an official visit to the university. In some cases, they may even invite you to attend the team's spring camp.

COACH BURRIS INSIGHT:

Start looking at the grade-point averages required to be accepted to university and compare them to your current grades. Once you have decided to pursue playing football at the post-secondary level, you need to give a 100 percent effort to achieve your goal.

ATHLETIC FINANCIAL AWARD

There is no such thing as a full athletic scholarship in Canadian university football where the university gives players fully paid tuition and room and board. Instead, we have the Athletic Financial Award (AFA).

There is an academic requirement that must be met to receive an AFA. Each university athletic conference has different educational requirements, so be sure to find out what these are for the school you decide to attend.

COACH BURRIS INSIGHT:

Players receiving an AFA will never see physical money in their hands. Instead, the student athlete will have a negative balance owing (or credit) on their student account until the end of the semester or year. Then, if the player meets the academic grade requirement, the AFA funds will be applied to the student athlete's school account.

EARN YOUR WORTH

You need to know how Canadian university football programs decide how much of an AFA they will offer you. The universities take into consideration your academic grades, how soon you will be contributing to the team, and your football abilities. Most Canadian university football programs have tight budgets, so you have to be an elite high school player, a top junior or CEGEP player recruit, or play games right away in your first year of university to earn the full amount of the AFA. *Earn* your Athletic Financial Award!

U SPORTS CENTRAL IDENTIFICATION NUMBER

U Sports has made an official registry to collect and track recruits and current players competing in U Sports. The goal for this registry is to let U Sports better understand its athletes. It is mandatory for every student athlete attending a Canadian university to register and have a U Sports Central Identification Number. Players are only required to register for a U Sports ID once during high school, and it costs $50 CAD. To register, go to usportscentral.ca/StudentCentre. On your U Sports profile, you can choose how interested football programs may contact you.

All players will need a U Sports ID to:

- Compete at the U Sports level
- Go on an official recruiting visit to a Canadian university campus
- Sign a letter of intent
- Track the number of official campus recruitment visits (maximum of five)
- Be informed about the recruiting process and athletic awards
- Help regulate and keep track of the recruiting process in Canadian university football

RECRUITING BLACKOUT PERIOD

U Sports has specific blackout periods for all Canadian university football programs. During these times, university coaches cannot contact or attempt to recruit players, as this would directly break recruiting rules.

U Sports Football Recruiting Blackout Dates[2]

Blackout Period	Dates	Explanation
Holiday blackout period	December 21–January 3	Holiday break
East-West blackout period	May 7–14	U Sports East-West All-Star Game and one full day following the completion of the game
July blackout period	July 1–31	Excluding the dates of the U18 Canada Cup tournament

COMMON MISTAKES

Some high school student athletes decide to attend university for the wrong reasons, such as:

1. Playing football without any desire to graduate. This is a *big* mistake. If you take away anything from this book, it should be to *never* go into financial debt just to play football.
2. Bending to social pressure. Some players want to attend university because their friends are.
3. Earning clout. Some players enjoy the football recruiting hype and the attention that comes in their final year of high school.
4. Waiting until Grade 12 to start the recruiting process. This is considered too late.

---

2 *Recruiting blackout dates can change, so be sure to do your research to confirm the dates.

5. Being afraid to contact coaches. Players should never be scared to contact the university and junior coaches when they require more information or clarity to make an educated recruiting decision.

6. Committing to the wrong program. Some student athletes choose a popular football program over the one that best suits them.

COACH BURRIS INSIGHT:

These common mistakes can be easily avoided. Take your time and do your research so you can make an informed decision.

U SPORTS FOOTBALL PROGRESSION

There are multiple progression options that players can take going the U Sports route.

- U Sports to junior football: Some players realize that playing university football is not for them and move to junior football.
- U Sports to NCAA: In unique situations, players start their post-secondary football careers in Canada and transfer to the NCAA Division 1 on a full scholarship.[1]
- U Sports to Professional football.

---

[1] Players at the U Sports level who have interest from a professional team will have the opportunity to be drafted or picked up as a free agent to play at the professional level.

NCAA FOOTBALL

As of January 2023, there has been major changes to initial eligibility requirement for the NCAA. The NCAA Divisions have removed the standardized testing, Scholastic Assessment Test (SAT) and the American College Testing (ACT) from their initial eligibility requirement. This does not mean that standardized testing is not required for admissions enrollment because some universities and colleges admissions requirements may require you to submit standardized test scores. It is strongly recommended that you check with each of the NCAA schools you are interested in and ask their admissions department if standardized testing is required. If it is not required, you do not need to write it for both NCAA eligibility and admission purposes.

Like me many years ago, I am sure most of you aspire to head to a favourite or top-tier NCAA or U Sports school. If you are in your junior year (Grade 11) or senior year (Grade 12) of high school, you might already be receiving interest from these schools and programs, plus others you may or may not have heard of or even considered. While this is an exciting time, you will need to remain focused on what is best for you. Going to a post-secondary school whose football team has consistently appeared in the playoffs or championship game the past ten years sounds great, but is it? Some critical questions you should ask yourself:

- **Who else are they recruiting for the position that I play?** Remember, most kids want to be recruited by top-ranked programs.
- **How do I compare skill-wise to other recruits?** You may be the best in your league, maybe even in your province, but for NCAA, you will be competing with others in Canada, the US, and a continuously growing international student athlete base.
- **How many players are in my position at that program, and what year are they in?** These are also the student athletes you will be competing against for a starting role, and it may limit your ability to either dress or get playing time if there is a large crop of rookie/sophomore student athletes.

- **Do I have any outside commitments that I'll need to maintain, and will the program be able to accept or assist with them?** A program with recruiting options may not be willing to help, or the program's time commitments may contrast with your personal ones.

While your goal may be to attend an NCAA school, you have more options than you think. For example, the NCAA has four different divisions: NCAA-IA, NCAA-IAA, NCAA-II, and NCAA-III.[3] Furthermore, you can remain in Canada to complete your studies and play U Sports, CEGEP, or junior football if your pursuit of playing NCAA-IA does not go as planned. As you can see, you have a lot of groundwork to cover researching which school/program you will want to attend, but the earlier you start, the better choice you'll make for yourself—not to mention that you'll be able to show recruiters your growth over time.

Before analyzing any programs with the above questions, you need to narrow down the schools you feel would be a good fit for you. Remember, this is about applying your talents to get an education and graduate debt-free. While I hope you reach your goal of playing professional football, understand that between the NFL and CFL there are roughly 2,200 active players, and most of them return the next year to play, so available spots are few. So graduating from university and having a high-quality education will allow you to have a smoother transition and take advantage of opportunities outside of football.

This process will take some time, and it should. Do not rush it. There are hundreds and hundreds of schools and programs throughout North America, and you need to be able to whittle them down to maybe twenty-five schools that are the top choices based on the criteria that are important to you. We have listed the criteria for consideration below.

Before we get to the list, it's important to note that your focus should be on the schools alone, if you are starting in Grades 9 or 10. You will have time

---

[3] www.ncaa.org/sports/2013/11/20/divisional-differences-and-the-history-of-multidivision-classification.aspx

to analyze the school academic programs later, around Grades 11 and 12, when they are more relevant to you. However, if you are starting late in this process, you'll need to do both right away, but start with the programs first.

If you are starting late in this process, you should be spending most of your efforts doing what this book outlines as requirements of recruitment—researching schools, editing and sending out your highlight tape, making contacts with coaches, visiting schools, etc.— instead of hanging out with friends. We understand this is your last year of high school, but your success moving forward is determined by your drive to succeed and accountability to your future success. You are already behind the eight-ball, and recruiters have been eying others for years and watching their growth as student athletes.

CRITERIA TO CONSIDER

The following are some important points you may want to consider as part of your research into each school and its football program:

School

Do you want to live at or away from home?

Do you want to stay in Canada or go to the US?

Do you want to stay in the province or go out of province (including the US)?

What undergrad program are you interested in? Does the school offer it, and are they known for it?

What is the size of the school you plan to attend? (Many large Canadian schools are only medium or small schools in NCAA-1A.)

What is the teacher-to-student ratio for the undergrad program you're interested in?

What type of community is around the school (rural, suburban, metropolitan)?

What kind of reputation does the institution have for the undergrad program you're interested in?

If you decide to live away, how much would it cost to travel home and back?

What school scholarships, bursaries, grants are available (if needed)?

Football program

What are the program's rankings?

How many student athletes play at your position?

What year are the student athletes at your position in (are they rookies, seniors)?

What are the football team's goals? Do they align with your football goals?

What are the rules of the program?

What is the size of the stadium? Can you play in front of 1,000 to 100,000 people? It can be intimidating.

What is the feeling you get from the head coach and position coach?

What vibe do you get from the players?

Is there a strong alumni presence? These could be connections to help with employment if the NFL/CFL isn't an option.

What are the program facilities like?

What athletic scholarships, bursaries, grants, etc. are available (if needed)?

Additional notes:

Remember, this is just a list of criteria we believe you should be considering when choosing a school and program. Some of these may not apply to you, or you may have other criteria not mentioned here that are important to you, so be sure to add these to your list. Your goal is to make sure that you not only go to a football program that suits you, but that you get the best possible education. If you have any unlisted criteria or unanswered questions, I encourage you to email me at coachburris@ironwillfootball.ca. I would love to help and answer them.

PROGRAM REQUIREMENTS FOR NCAA SCHOOLS

Taking the next step to post-secondary school can be scary, especially when you're just entering Grade 9. But with this book in hand, you're already on your way to making your transition from high school to post-secondary school as smooth as possible, as long as you put in the effort and are proactive.

The NCAA has strict guidelines around which student athletes get accepted. See below for a timeline on when you should be completing tasks. Please note this is not all-encompassing; you should review all material provided by the NCAA Eligibility Center when you create your profile page. The online registration process at the NCAA Eligibility Center requires you to set up a profile page: web3.ncaa.org/ecwr3/register/CERTIFICATION

High school timeline for NCAA enrolment	
Grade 9 - Plan	**Grade 10 - Register**
• You should start your planning here. You need to make sure you are taking the right courses (see credit requirement table) and getting the best grades (do no fool around). • Make sure you review the academic guidelines the NCAA has for Canada and the course titles that are approved as credits. • Sign up for a free profile page account at eligiblitycenter.org where you can get information on the requirements you must fulfill.	• At this point you want to make sure you are registered and have a profile page or certification account with NCAA Eligibility Center. • Continue to monitor your Eligibility Center account for any updates and further steps you may need to follow. • **DO NOT** take shortcuts if you have fallen behind. Use the worksheets available to help get you back on course and monitor your progress towards meeting the requirements.
Grade 11 - Study	**Grade 12 - Graduate**
• Make time to check in with your guidance counsellor or an education assistant who knows and understands the process and can make sure you are still on track to graduate on time and with the required credits. • Prepare for and take your SAT/ACT test and submit it to your NCAA Eligibility Center account. • Manage your account including your sports participation page and make sure all information is correct. • Make sure all transcripts are submitted to the Eligibility Center from your school(s). If you go to more than one school, transcripts will be required for each.	• Redo your SAT/ACT exams if you did not do well the first time, and resubmit scores to the Eligibility Center. • Make sure you request your final amateurism certification on April 1 (for fall enrollees, and Oct 1 for winter enrollees). This should be done through the Eligibility Center page. • After you graduate, you will need to ask your school(s) to submit your final official transcript with proof of graduation to the Eligibility Center.

Retrieved from http://fs.ncaa.org
Note: Completing the credits based on Division I will allow you to be accepted into Division II schools, but completing Div. II credits may not get you into Div. I schools. We recommend you complete the credits based on Div. I standards.

As a part of this timeline, you need to make sure you are taking the right classes, the ones that will give you the credits required to satisfy the NCAA requirements for sixteen core courses to be accepted to a Division I or Division II school. Please review the table below, as the requirements between the two divisions are slightly different.

Division I NCAA School					
The following 16 core course credits will need to be completed in order to be accepted to schools in this division.					
4 Credits	**3 Credits**	**2 Credits**	**1 Credit**	**2 Credits**	**4 Credits**
English/native language	Math	Natural/physical science	Additional (English or native language, math, or natural/physical science)	Social science	Additional courses (any area listed to the left, foreign language or comparative religion, philosophy)
Division II NCAA School					
The following 16 core course credits will need to be completed in order to be accepted to schools in this division.					
3 Credits	**2 Credits**	**2 Credits**	**3 Credit**	**2 Credits**	**4 Credits**
English/lative language	Math	Natural/physical science	Additional (English or native language, math, or natural/physical science)	Social science	Additional courses (any area listed to the left, foreign language or comparative religion, philosophy)

Retrieved from https://www.ncaa.org/student-athletes/future/core-courses
Note: Provinces use different ways to determine what is considered a full credit so, please review the Guide to International Academic Standards, select Canada, and review your province's criteria.

While our objective is to give you the best information possible, please make sure to review your Eligibility Center page and any other resources provided in this book to ensure you are on track.

The NCAA monitors your performance from each grade level, so don't wait until Grade 11 or 12 to focus on your academics; that is a recipe for failure.

LATE TO THE GAME

Hopefully, you are preparing for the next stage before you reach Grade 11. If you are entering Grade 12 and just starting to consider NCAA as an option, you're going to have to work a bit harder. Even still, be sure to do the following as soon as possible:

1. Immediately make an appointment with a guidance counsellor to discuss where you currently stand compared to what has been provided above (you may be on track without even knowing it).
2. Register with the NCAA Eligibility Center and review its material, and make sure to bring everything requested to your appointment with your guidance counsellor.
3. Use the worksheet to help get you back on track with your guidance counsellor's assistance. This may require summer school, but it's a small price to pay to reach your football dreams.
4. Reach out to the Eligibility Center with any additional questions or concerns you may have, as there might be alternatives available for you, depending on your situation.
5. Whatever you do, tell potential coaches who may be interested in recruiting you that you have started the recruiting process late. Tell them what you are doing to catch up and get in front of the situation, so come graduation you are ready.

If you are too far behind, you still have options. You can forego the NCAA and focus on Canadian universities, or join a junior program or CEGEP team. This will allow you to finish your requirements, and it will give you another year to apply to the NCAA. Some coaches from the NCAA may request you do this to develop your skills or to get more game film so they can re-evaluate your game performance.

Another option is to try transferring from a Canadian university to the NCAA. If you do this, you may be required to sit out one year and lose that amount of eligibility. Furthermore, if you decide to go this route, make sure the NCAA school and coach are both on board and you fulfill all requirements and obligations needed for the transfer. Check out the transfer eligibility requirements from the "Already a Student in University" section of the Eligibility Center.

NCAA TIPS

If your Plan A is to play at the NCAA level, keep pursuing that option, but keep your options with Canadian universities open. Many players make the mistake of shutting down any interest from Canadian programs while pursuing their NCAA dream. The key takeaway here is to *never burn bridges.*

Another mistake some players make is trying to get recruited by the biggest and most popular schools in the NCAA. Understand that the NCAA has a variety of conferences. You might gain more attention and have a better chance of being offered a full scholarship from smaller Div I schools in small conferences. For example, my friend went to the Ohio State summer football camp and ran a 4.3 forty-yard dash time on a pulled hamstring. He was offered a full scholarship right on the spot. He ended up signing with the Ohio State Buckeyes. During his time at Ohio State, he saw limited playing time. He suffered injuries, and the competition was intense. He ended up transferring to a small Div I school, where he found more success and playing time. The point is you want to choose the school that is the right fit for you, one that offers you a good chance of earning playing time. Going to the most popular schools is not always the best fit for you as a football player.

NCAA football is a huge business for the universities and colleges; the priority is to win football games, championships, and bowl games. Coaches are more demanding, and players are held accountable for their actions on and off the field. Most football programs operate with the next-man-up mentality; meaning, if you cannot get the job done on the football field, you will not see playing time or will be out-recruited.

NCAA FOOTBALL PROGRESSION

There are multiple progression options that players can take going the NCAA football route.

- NCAA football to U Sports: There are situations wherein players start their post-secondary football career on a NCAA university team and transfer back to a Canadian team.
- NCAA football to professional football

Note: Players at the NCAA level who have generated interest from professional teams will have the opportunity to be drafted, or picked up as a free agent to play at the professional level.

CANADIAN JUNIOR FOOTBALL LEAGUE (CJFL)

The CJFL reaches from Ontario to British Columbia. Players cannot turn twenty-three years old during the current calendar year; only players twenty-two years old and under can compete. It provides numerous benefits and advantages to players looking to play competitive football after high school. The junior football level is in between high and university football.

> *Junior football allowed me the opportunity to get playing time right away, which contributed to my development as a player. Playing junior can be just as good a start to your career as going to a university and redshirting for a year, and that two-year window before your "clock" starts certainly helps. Junior football taught me to work hard for my goals. After year two of junior, I realized that playing university football was a possibility once universities started reaching out to me.*

Theren Churchill, 2020 Toronto Argonauts' ninth pick overall
Regina Rams, Edmonton Huskies

WHY PLAY JUNIOR FOOTBALL?

Junior football provides a higher level of coaching and competition than high school. Using junior football as a steppingstone to playing university football is a great option. It allows players to develop positional skills, mature mentally as a football player, develop strength and speed from off-season programs, and compete at a higher level on the field.

Players can enroll in college or university and still play two years of junior football before their U Sports eligibility clock starts. Some players take university courses and play junior football until they are ready to play U Sports football. Players can enter U Sports with two academic years completed and still have five years of eligibility.

There are student athletes graduating from high school who still do not know what they want to pursue academically in college or university. That's fine, as players can play junior football and join the workforce until they decide what they want to pursue academically. Why waste hard-earned money on tuition fees when you are undecided about your academic passion?

With junior football, you play more live games than a redshirt freshman or a second-year player who can't crack the university game dress roster. So, ask yourself: Who is getting better and playing more football, junior players or U Sports players?

U Sports coaches use junior football as a recruiting resource. You are more likely to play right away in U Sports after playing junior football, because coaches know the level of competition is higher than at the high school level.

DECIDING TO PLAY JUNIOR FOOTBALL

If you are not 100 percent sure which junior football program you want to play for, do not give a verbal commitment to a junior program until you're entirely sure that the team is the right fit for you. Once you know how much time you would like to commit, sign the letter of intent on the national signing day on June 1.

The best plan of attack when deciding which junior program is the right fit for you is by attending the junior football program spring camps of the teams that have interest in you. This way you will get a feel for the program, how the team operates, the coaching staff, and your potential teammates. Once you have attended these camps, you will be able to make an informed decision.

Keep in mind, however, that you will need to coordinate the dates of each spring camp. Depending on the camp dates, you might be playing a lot of football in a short amount of time. So, it's important to be in top physical condition by spring.

COACH BURRIS INSIGHT:

If you are thinking about going back to high school to upgrade your academics and to play football to get more game film to play university football, you may want to consider playing junior football instead. University coaches would rather see you play a year of junior football and compete at a higher level than playing another year of high school football.

JUNIOR FOOTBALL PROGRESSION

There are multiple progression options that players can take going the junior football route.

- Canadian Junior Football League
- Canadian Junior Football League to U Sports
- Canadian Junior Football League to U Sports to professional football
- Canadian Junior Football League to NCAA to professional football
- Canadian Junior Football League to professional football

CEGEP AND CEGEP FOOTBALL

CEGEP is a two-year pre-university program that is mandatory for Quebec students who want to attend university. These students will receive a diploma of collegial studies. CEGEP football is similar to junior football, a league between high school and university football, but it is only played in the province of Quebec. The difference between junior and CEGEP football is that, in CEGEP, you must be enrolled at the CEGEP college and be a student to play football. If you're a student athlete who does not speak French, you can only attend the English-speaking schools: Champlain College in Lennoxville or Vanier College in Montreal.

WHY PLAY CEGEP FOOTBALL?

- Players who live outside of Quebec will go to CEGEP to upgrade their academics and move to the university level.
- Players who are close to signing an NCAA scholarship will go to CEGEP to play football at a higher competition level to gain film with the intent of earning an NCAA scholarship.

- Out-of-province players can gain more exposure playing in the CEGEP league because the competition level is higher than high school. When coaches are scouting players, they want to know that the player is competing against good competition.
- Some players play CEGEP because they are undecided about the academic and/or football direction they want to take. CEGEP allows players to mature and determine their best direction.

CEGEP FOOTBALL PROGRESSION

There are multiple progression options that players can take when going the CEGEP football route.

- CEGEP
- CEGEP to U Sports
- CEGEP to NCAA
- CEGEP to U Sports/NCAA to professional level

NATIONAL JUNIOR COLLEGE ATHLETIC ASSOCIATION (NJCAA)

Junior colleges are in the United States. They are two-year post-secondary institutions that provide academic education and training for individuals who want to pursue careers after junior college.

WHY ATTEND JUNIOR COLLEGE?

- Players are academically ineligible to play in the NCAA and need to upgrade their academics.
- They need more game film.
- They need to develop as an athlete.
- Another way of obtaining scholarships at the division level.

NATIONAL JUNIOR COLLEGE ATHLETIC ASSOCIATION PROGRESSION

There are multiple progression options that players can take when going the Junior College football route.

- Junior college
- Junior college to NCAA
- Junior college to U Sports
- Junior college to NCAA/U Sports to professional level

POST-SECONDARY FOOTBALL BREAKDOWN

Post-secondary football leagues	Academics enrollment required	Progression to professional level CFL/NFL/ Europe	Scholarships and financial awards	Team tryouts
U Sports Canadian university football	Yes	Yes	Athletic Financial Award	Yes
NCAA football	Yes	Yes	Scholarships	Yes
Canadian Junior Football League	No	Yes	Depending on the organization	Yes
CEGEP football	Yes	No	No	Yes
National Junior College Athletic Association	Yes	No	Yes, but schools vary from state to state in financial support, from full scholarships to partial scholarships.	Yes

CHAPTER 3

Recruitment

To be successfully recruited and not left behind, you need to understand how the recruiting process works. High school players who are extremely talented will be the top priority on university and junior programs' recruiting boards and will be aggressively recruited. These players will have less to worry about when it comes to generating recruiting exposure.

A key point for you to understand: Canadian universities and NCAA football programs work one year ahead in their recruiting process. For example, the various football programs complete 2030 recruiting in 2029. In 2030, the team focus is on signing the 2030 recruiting class and working toward recruiting 2031. So, coaches are identifying and evaluating the players in Grade 11. From there, their focus is on signing those players in their Grade 12 year. As such, your Grade 11 year is critical when it comes to football recruiting.

GETTING NOTICED

There are many ways in which university and junior teams will identify you as a potential recruit. Head coaches and recruiters are everywhere. Below are the most common ways a team will find you.

- Head coaches and recruiting coordinators will be at local games, playoff games, championships, and even your team practice. Many coaches and recruiters prefer to blend in and not attract any attention, as it allows them to evaluate players anonymously.
- Recruiting coaches will identify you if you participate in any football combine events or elite team tryouts. Keep in mind

that some of these coaches are the ones running drills, so it's a perfect opportunity for them to see you in action. If they like your skill set, they may ask for your contact information.

- Coaches will be watching you if you play on elite teams, such as provincials or Team Canada.
- If you send your film directly to junior and university coaches and they like your skill set, they will reach out to you.
- Believe it or not, coaches might even find you on someone else's highlight tape or game film. You might catch the coach's attention, which will have them looking for film on you as well. When the bright lights are on, be sure you are at your best. You never know which coaches are looking at the film and scouting you.
- Coaches will watch a lot of game and highlight film on Hudl, an online video analysis platform.
- Your head coach might recommend you to university and junior football programs.
- Coaches often find recruits from current players on the team, who recommend their friends to the coaching staff if they think they are good enough to play at that specific level.

STARTING THE RECRUITING PROCESS

An essential part of the process is understanding what university football coaches and recruiting coordinators are initially looking for when recruiting a player out of high school. This information will help you eliminate a lot of wasted time and enable you to only focus on what is important.

University recruiters and coaches are interested in the following:

- graduation year
- academic grades
- film
- personal character

The recruiting process will only go forward if the head coach and recruiting coordinator like your film and you're academically strong. Coaches may also want to know your injury history, feedback from your high school coaches, your field performance, and how you are as a teammate.

It is simple to start the recruiting process: make a phone call to the head coach or recruiting coordinator. In this call, you can introduce yourself and let them know what school you attend, your position, and your graduation year. If a phone call feels intimidating, you can send a short email with this information. Coaches are busy, so avoid writing a long email because they may not have time to read it. You can also add a short highlight clip or clips—no more than a minute long. Your email subject heading should be well thought out to grab the coach's attention.

THE COMMUNICATION PROCESS

1. **Initial communication:** Write a brief letter or make a phone call with the aforementioned details.
2. **Follow up:** Depending on the coaches' preferred method of contact (text, phone, email, etc.), follow up with them after your initial contact. For example, if the coach gets back to you via text, follow up through text.
3. **Follow up again:** You should follow up with coaches as often as you need to.

The recruiting process has changed drastically from twenty years ago. Players would edit their highlight tape on VHS cassette, write a cover letter for their football résumé, and then mail that package to university and college coaches. This process was costly, and you never knew if the coaches even received your film.

I am happy that players today do not have to go through that process. Technology and the internet have made things a lot easier for players. Social media platforms make it effortless for players to reach out to coaches, and vice versa. Editing and making a highlight tape today is user-friendly and straightforward. Players can use platforms such as Hudl to make their highlight tapes and post and share them with coaches, teammates, and friends, which is so much easier and more efficient. To learn how to put together your highlight tape, read Chapter 7: How to Make a Highlight Tape.

Because it is easier for coaches and players to connect through social media, all players need to start the recruiting process are their academic transcripts, which year they will be graduating from high school, and their game film. From there, coaches can determine if players would be able get into their school and evaluate their film to see if they are potential recruits.

If players decide to go another route, where academics are not required (like playing junior football), coaches will just need to evaluate the film. All you need to know is when and where to send your film and how to contact coaches. This information can all be found on the team's website.

RESEARCHING THE RECRUITS

University coaches do a lot of background research on recruits to learn who the player really is. They want to bring in players of high skill and character, but the player must be the right fit for their program. The team culture of a program is what wins championships, and if a player compromises it, the recruiting stops.

Players must understand that when coaches do checkups, they want to find out what type of person you are, not how good a player you are. They specifically want to know about your attitude, character, and work ethic, and what are you like when you're away from the football field. Post-secondary coaches will talk to your head coach, assistant coaches, guidance counsellors, teachers, and even opposing coaches. It all depends on how deep the team wants to dive to find out what type of person you are.

As a student athlete, you work so hard in the classroom and as an athlete, so the last thing you want is to have character issues that force post-secondary football programs to walk away from you.

THE HIGHS AND LOWS OF THE RECRUITING PROCESS

As much fun as the recruiting process is, most people only visualize the glory of going on campus visits and signing the letter of intent and never imagine or understand what most players go through to get to that point. It's an emotional roller coaster.

It's a unique situation to be in, because players never know what a coach or university recruiter is thinking. You're trying to make a good impression without deterring the coaches so they move on to another recruit. For example, it is common to have a football program contact you by a coach who is excited during the conversation, telling you the team wants to bring you in for a visit, but then, for some reason, you never hear back from that coach again.

You might receive a lot of interest from every program *except* the one you want to play in, despite continued efforts to contact the coach. There's also the possibility of not receiving a full Athletic Financial Award or scholarship because they do not see the potential required for full funding. Even the highs you get when every school in the country has serious interest in you as a player can take their toll. These are all examples of the highs and lows that make up the turbulent seas of the recruiting process.

I conducted a number of interviews and discussions with players and coaches from high school, junior football, U Sports, and NCAA Division I. Here is a short list of what they enjoyed most about the recruiting process.

- Seeing the hard work pay off and receiving recruiting calls from university and junior coaches.
- Receiving the first offer.

- Seeing high school players improve their grades because of their passion for football.
- Increased self-confidence and motivation to improve when coaches called to recruit.
- Learning more about the game by, for example, taking video calls with coaches and watching and breaking down practice and game film.
- The positive attention received from coaches when being recruited.
- Being wanted by a team and knowing they were looking out for the players' best interests.

COACH BURRIS INSIGHT:

It's important not to get caught up in the roller coaster, to never let your emotions get too high or low. The process can be draining and cause you to become distracted and lose focus. Keep your emotions balanced and enjoy the ride.

AM I BEING RECRUITED?

A lot of players I have worked with have a hard time gauging if a football program is serious about recruiting. Players get confused because they may receive light interest, like a phone call from coaches, generic emails, or physical mail from football programs. The following will help you understand if a post-secondary football program is serious about recruiting:

Please check the boxes that apply to you:

Signs that will let you know if a team is serious about recruiting you:	
You've received phone calls, texts, video invites, or video-call requests from the head coach or the recruiting coordinator. Listen for their tone and level of enthusiasm during the conversation.	☐
A coach calls with personalized football recruiting information, or sends handwritten invitations to camps.	☐
The head coach or recruiting coordinator goes above and beyond expectations and is accommodating.	☐
The coach attends games or practices.	☐
You're invited on an official campus visit.	☐
The coach schedules a home visit.	☐
Coaches continue to keep in contact after you have sent your academic transcripts.	☐
Coaches contact your present coach to find out more about you.	☐
Coaches ask for additional film.	☐

THE POINT OF CONTACT

When teams begin to show interest in you, there will be a few individuals you should expect to have conversations with. The decision-maker on the football team is the head coach, and you will most likely have numerous conversations with them. The recruiting coordinator will also play a significant role during the process, as they will be evaluating your grades, talking to your high school coach, setting up your campus visit, and answering all your questions.

You will communicate with your positional coaches as well. This will be a great opportunity to learn more about your positional unit, your coach's expectations, and how they operate. Lastly, you might have some communication with current players on the team. It is important to know who you will be interacting with and what their role on the team is.

Please check the boxes that apply to you:

How to know when you're not being seriously recruited:	
You only receive generic emails and letters from the football program.	☐
You haven't received phone calls, texts, video invites, or video-call requests from the program's coaches or recruiting coordinator.	☐
Coaches won't return your phone calls or reply to your emails.	☐
You only receive non-football recruiting-related information that promotes the school and why you should attend their university.	☐
Coaches haven't asked you for academic transcripts.	☐
You receive mass emails from the football program but have not received any personalized communication for the school itself.	☐
Additional notes:	

If there are no signs of interest from the school of your choice, I highly recommend being persistent and reaching out to the head coach or recruiting coordinator to express your interest in being a part of their football program. Contacting the coaches is also beneficial because it allows you to ask additional questions about their program to find out if you have any interest in becoming a player on the team.

HOW TO GAIN FREE EXPOSURE

Don't be like me and shell out money for expensive marketing and recruiting agencies when you can gain exposure on your own for free. The reality is that the majority of the recruiting services will sell you the dream, or make you feel incapable of getting recruited without their help. Keep in mind that when you really want something bad enough, your emotions will pull you in and you end up making knee-jerk decisions, which can cost you money.

One of the easiest and most accessible ways to reach out to junior and university coaches is online. Most junior and university football websites have a recruiting link with a questionnaire and a place to add your highlight tape link. This can all be filled out online in a matter of minutes.

Here are a few suggestions for filling out the online questionnaire:

- Be honest when answering.
- Answer all of the questions.
- Make sure you put together an organized highlight tape. You will want to grab the coach's attention by front-loading your highlight tape with your best plays. Note: For more details, read Chapter 7: How to Make a Highlight Tape.

COACH BURRIS INSIGHT:

When I coached university football, one of my responsibilities was checking the online recruiting inbox and reviewing all the completed questionnaires and videos for the position I coached. If the film wasn't clear or the questionnaire wasn't fully completed, I moved on to the next player.

Most Canadian university, junior football, CEGEP, junior college and NCAA football programs have online recruiting information and forms that high school players can fill out. This information will go directly to the head coach or the recruiting coordinator.

The photos below will show you how to access the recruiting form. Simply go to the football program's website and look for the "recruiting" or "recruitment" links.

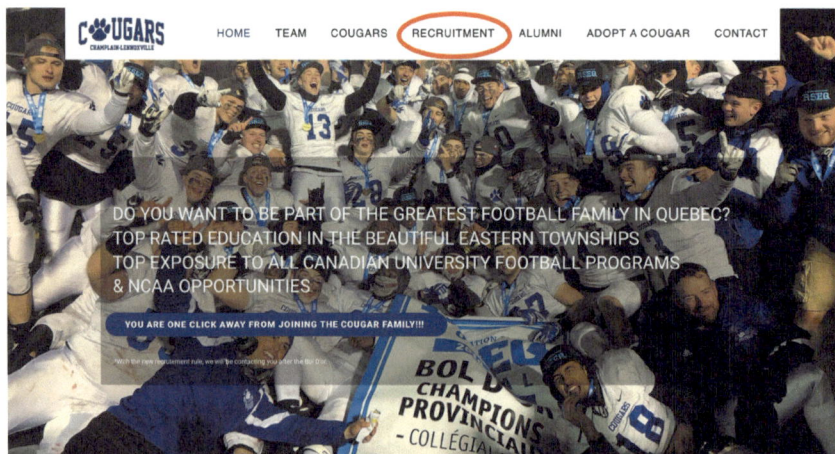

Once you are directed to the recruitment page, read all of the provided recruiting information. Look for a link that says "Fill out recruitment form."

COACH BURRIS INSIGHT:

Each football program is different, so look for recruiting in the menu bar. This is one of the best ways to generate exposure.

HOW TO MARKET YOURSELF

Gaining exposure is a hot topic for players who want to play football after high school. The best exposure will depend on your game-day performance and how you perform at university camps where coaches can see you in person. The players who perform at a high level will have no problem attracting coaches' attention at the post-secondary level.

I am not saying players who do not have their best season can't make it at the junior or university level, but it will take a lot more work to attract their attention.

The best way to gain attention is to follow the action steps laid out in the previous sections. In addition, you should be posting the following on major social media platforms.

Social media exposure points
An organized highlight tape. Read Chapter 7: How to Make a Highlight Tape for details
Any training clips in which you hit a personal best
Anything that showcases your football skills
Anything that highlights your athletic talent (e.g., dunking a basketball, sprinting 100 metres, hitting a personal best in the weight room)

Be sure to tag and directly message coaches any clips or new academic and athletic accomplishments. Use hashtags directed to the football program of interest. Emailing and calling coaches are also effective, as their contact information is made public on the team website.

HOW TO BE RECRUITED WITH LIMITED FILM

The best way for coaches to see you in action if you have limited film is by going to football camps, specifically university summer camps. Go to as many university, private, and provincial tryout camps as possible. You will learn from and be coached by some of the teams' coaching staff, and again, the coaches will see you and your ability firsthand.

Private camps allow you to develop your football skills and receive good coaching. The top private camps in the country will have a solid staff that includes coaches who work at the junior and university levels.

WHY UNIVERSITY COACHES MAY NOT RESPOND

One of the main reasons players give up on their dreams of playing college football is that they do not hear back from coaches or recruiting coordinators after sending in their tapes. Don't give up. There are several contributing factors as to why you may not have heard back, such as:

- **The time of year:** U Sports and the NCAA have specific times throughout the year when they cannot contact recruits (see recruiting blackout periods in Chapter 1).
- **Your age:** If you're a fifteen-year-old player who sent in your highlight tape, you may not receive a call or email because coaches are focused on signing the current recruiting class.
- **Too busy:** Coaches are sometimes so focused on the task at hand that they simply forget to return calls or emails.
- **Poor organization:** Coaches and recruiting coordinators are human too. Sometimes their organizational skills are not the best, and they may drop the ball with returning calls or emails.

Of course, the quality of your film, your grades, and your graduating year may also be factors that contribute to a lack of response from coaches. Follow up with team coaches if you do not receive a response.

GRABBING THEIR ATTENTION

Coaches would always rather see the athletes in live action than through film. This gives the recruiters and coaches the opportunity to evaluate the player's performance and how they interact with their teammates and coaches.

Other ways to grab the attention of the coaches include:

- Attending combine events where university and college coaches will be in attendance
- Attending performance camps
- Participating in 7-on-7 tournaments
- Attending linemen showcase events
- Trying out for elite-level football teams

THE BENEFITS OF PLAYING ON PROVINCIAL AND NATIONAL TEAMS

Playing football on the provincial team, competing in the Canada Cup, playing for Team Canada, and being a part of the International Bowl team are all excellent ways to represent your province and country— and they come with significant benefits. As a positional coach on the Alberta U18 team for three years, I have seen firsthand how players have benefited from being on these teams.

The Canada Cup is the elite-level tournament for high school football players under eighteen years old. Each province in Canada is represented and competes for the tournament championship. The International Bowl team is made up of the best players from the Canada Cup tournament. They will compete for Team Canada and play multiple games against teams from all over the world. The International Bowl is held in Texas.

Before covering these benefits, I want to address a common question:

> *If my son doesn't make the provincial team, does that mean*
> *he is not good enough to play post-secondary football?*

The answer is *no*. Plenty of players do not make the provincial team but go on to have successful collegiate football careers, and some even move on to the professional ranks. So, don't panic if your son doesn't make the provincial team.

There are numerous benefits to playing for a provincial or national team. These teams help players gain exposure, resulting in higher chances of being recruited. Every player is encouraged to try out for their provincial team, at least.

- **Exposure:** The exposure players receive at the Canada Cup and on the national team is tremendous. In the Canada Cup, you play in front of university coaches from across Canada. This is an opportunity for players in remote areas to gain significant exposure and make a name for themselves. Remote players have often used this to their advantage because they do not have the same opportunities as players in a high-exposure school. If they excel in national tournaments like the Canada Cup, they have a greater chance of making a provincial team.

- **Competition:** At the U18 Canada Cup and the International Bowl, players compete against the best players in their age group, so their competition level will never be in question. They can also use their game-day performance as a measuring stick against the rest of the competition.
- **Film:** Players will also benefit from the film quality and the correct filming angles that are used to film the games at the U18 Canada Cup and the International Bowl games. Players gain access to the game film for study and use in their highlight tapes.

SUMMER CAMPS, COMBINES, AND SHOWCASE EVENTS

Summer camps, combines, and showcase events are critical to helping players learn, develop, and demonstrate their football talents. The time constraints of fall football season practices and game planning don't leave much time for skill development. The off-season is when players need to develop their skills, and that is why football camp, combines, and showcase events are so important. Be sure to take the time to research and plan which summer activities you are interested in attending. This will help provide you with exposure and develop your football skills.

COACH BURRIS INSIGHT:

It is important to understand the different types of camp offerings, because each camp serves a specific purpose. You could be a player looking to develop your football skills at a skills camp and end up registering a showcase event or combine, expecting to learn more in-depth football skills and being disappointed because you registered for the wrong camp type.

THINGS TO THINK ABOUT

Do you want to play Canadian university football U Sports? Or play NCAA Division 1 football in the United States?

To get the best opportunity and gain exposure at the U Sports Canadian university level, attend the school's football camps and their prospect football camp events. Coaches at the U Sports and NCAA level want to see you in person. You are evaluated and measured by your performance at camp.

COACH BURRIS INSIGHT:

Suggestion for planning your summer football camp tour: Whether it be U Sports or NCAA camp, go to two camps of your dream schools and two camps that you know you will generate a lot of interest.

Do you want to travel around Canada or the United States and attend different university football summer camps and combines?

To ensure that you get in front of the right coaches, the majority of the camps you attend should be university camps. Remember, the objective of attending these camps is exposure and development. Private camps are great as well, but they focus on development rather than exposure.

Attending camps, showcases, and combine events allows you to compete against solid competition.

Engaging in high-end competition will allow you to gauge your own talent level, which can help direct which football pathway you should take after high school.

PERFORMANCE SKILL CAMPS

Players who attend performance skill camps are interested in improving and developing their skills and knowledge for long-term athletic development, positional technique, overall football skills, and building football intelligence. These camps are generally three to five full days in length.

COMBINES AND SHOWCASE EVENTS

At a combine, players will go through multiple drills to test their overall athleticism, strength, and speed. In Canada, organized combine events happen more often than showcase events.

Attending football combines while in high school is another great way to gain exposure and get in front of university and junior coaches. The main objective of the combine is to test the players' overall athleticism. Players will participate in a variety of athletic drills: running the 40-, 20-, and 10-yard dash, shuttle agility and three-cone-drill agility, and 225 bench press or push-ups, depending on the age level of the combine. Players will be tested on their lower-body explosiveness through the broad jump or vertical test. Some combines will include a competition session, where linemen will compete in one-on-one pass-rush run drills, and skill positions will compete with pass one-on-ones.

COACH BURRIS INSIGHT:

A great way to figure out the best combines and showcase events to attend is to look for the ones where university or college coaches will be present.

Coaches want to see you perform, so be sure to dominate each combine event. Players who are physically prepared test well at the combine and find success at these events. Testing well is everything, because coaches who are unable to attend the combine event will still receive the players' results. If your combine result numbers do not stand out, coaches will overlook you.

COACH BURRIS INSIGHT:

If you have not trained for the basic combine events, you should carefully consider if it's worth attending, because combines are based on how well you test. Make sure you physically prepared for the combine if you plan to participate.

At a showcase event, players will do position-specific dills and have positional competition. For example, showcase events will have positional drills and then move on to competition drills like one-on-ones with receivers and defensive backs, or one-on-ones with offensive and defensive linemen. Showcase events mainly happen in the United States, and allows university coaches to see players live and in action.

Players go to showcase events and combines to gain exposure and show off their skills. There is not much football teaching at these events, but there is a lot of player vs. player competition and many competition drills. Coaches who lead these events will explain and lead the drills or competition, and then players must execute them to the best of their abilities. This is an excellent opportunity to see where you match up against elite talent. Normally, post-secondary coaches will attend showcase events, so it's a great way to meet them and talk about recruiting.

It's important to have a "shark" mindset when participating at showcase and combine events. This means you have an appetite for success, and you will not let anything get in the way of your prey— your potential recruitment. Be sure to get as many reps as possible at each drill. The more reps you get in each drill, the more coaches can see you in action and evaluate you. You want to make a lasting impression on the coaches, so stand out and make the most of the extra reps with explosive plays. However, be sure to stay coachable. Execute each drill exactly as requested.

UNIVERSITY CAMPS

University camps, which take place on campus, are a fantastic opportunity to perform in front of university football coaches who will work with you and evaluate your skills. The university that hosts the camp has their own staff and players to coach. It is common for participants who perform well at university camps to attract the university team's attention and sometimes receive offers.

COACH BURRIS INSIGHT:

If your goal is to play post-secondary football in the United States, I recommend attending American university camps to help showcase your talents and generate exposure. The best way to generate exposure and increase your chances of receiving a scholarship offer is to be seen in person and perform well at the camps.

CELEBRITY FOOTBALL CAMPS

Celebrity football camps are a great opportunity to meet professional football players and learn from them. These types of camps offer low to no exposure for players, but they provide skills and drills development.

Camp Type	Positional skill coaching	Player talent evaluation and ranking	Exposure level
Performance and skills camp	Yes	No	Low/medium
Combines and showcase events	Medium	Yes	High
University football camps	Yes	No	High
Celebrity football camps	Yes	No	Low

COACH BURRIS INSIGHT:

Do your research. You will want to attend the football camp that best aligns with your goals. You can call or email the camp director or event organizer to find out more information to ensure the specific camp is the right fit.

YOUR COACHES ARE A RECRUITING RESOURCE

Your high school and community coaches can be valuable resources when it comes to recruiting and getting you to the next level. Here's how they can help.

- **Bridging the gap:** Your high school coach can bridge the gap between the high school player and the university or junior coach. University coaches rely on your coaches' feedback about your skills and character. You will gain a lot more interest if your high school coach recommends you to football programs at the next level.

- **Education and insight:** Your high school coach can also educate you and provide insight into the recruiting process and how it works. The recruiting process is always changing, and your coach should be familiar with deadline dates or any university or eligibility rule changes. Some coaches go as far as providing players with information on which football camps and tryouts to attend.
- **Gain exposure:** High school coaches can also help create exposure for you by contacting post-secondary teams on your behalf, and your coach can write reference letters and send your film to teams so they can evaluate your skills. The football community is small, and many coaches have built relationships with post-secondary coaches all over Canada. Being able to tap into their network of post-secondary coaches can help you get to the next level.

Your high school coach should be your first call when you begin your recruiting process and are learning how to gain exposure. When I went through the recruiting process, I expressed my interest in playing football beyond high school to my coach. He was very supportive, and provided insight and support that helped get the ball rolling. Initially, my coach made a few calls to the network of coaches he knew at the university level, and he wrote reference letters for me. After that, it was up to me.

Your high school coach is not an agent or a recruiting service. I continued to reach out to schools and send in my film. Stay proactive throughout the recruiting process, even if your coaches say they will help you. If you're engaging yourself in the recruiting process and your coach is helping as well, it's a win-win. Don't put your future into someone else's hands. You have to take ownership of your future and take the necessary steps to achieve your goals.

CHAPTER 4
The Blueprint Checklist

This is an essential section. The player and parent research that was done to complete this book showed that players and parents had limited understanding of recruiting, how and when to start the process, and what needs to be accomplished throughout high school. This blueprint will walk you through the process, starting from Grade 9 all the way to Grade 12.

The purpose of this section is to keep you on schedule and focused on tasks you need to accomplish in a specific timeline. In addition, the blueprint will outline your objectives and what to expect from grade to grade.

I wish I had this section when I was going through the recruiting process.

GRADE 9 ACTION PLAN AND TO-DO CHECKLIST

Even though you're still a few years away from finishing high school, you can do things to set yourself up for graduation.

OBJECTIVES

As a Grade 9 student athlete, this is the time to explore your passions and interests, and find out your strengths as an individual. You should be in research mode. Look into the different leagues at the post-secondary level, explore football programs that interest you, and check out the rosters. Be sure to review their academic requirements as well. The more research you do in Grade 9, the better understanding you will have about how recruiting works, and the more prepared you will be to make educated decisions.

Here are a few suggested steps and tasks you should take if you are considering playing football after high school. After each task, there is a suggested timeframe to complete each step.

Grade 9 tasks and description	Time of year to execute
Personal	
After the fall season, use the off-season to figure out if being a student athlete and pursuing football after high school graduation is something you want to do. Secondly, you will want to ask yourself, *Am I ready to be a student athlete?* **Hint:** Start looking at the grade-point averages required to be accepted to university and compare your current grades to those. Once you have decided to pursue playing football at the post-secondary level, you need to give 100-percent effort to achieve your goal.	November– August
Learn and develop good time management and study skills. If needed, consult your head coach or guidance counsellor for time management and studying strategies. You will want to master both these skills to succeed in university and in life.	All year
Academics	
Take care of your academics! • Attend class regularly. • Complete all homework and assignments. • Seek academic support if needed. Take advantage of tutorial time at school; teachers are available to help students before and after school and at lunch.	September– June
Meet with your guidance counsellor at least twice during the academic year or as needed to figure out what core courses are required, and to set up an academic schedule to meet university and/or college academic requirements.	September– November
Research	
Research and learn about the different football options available to you upon high school graduation. Questions: • What leagues can I play after high school? U Sports, junior football, CEGEP, junior college, and the NCAA. • Do I need academics to play at that level? If academics are required, look into the entry-level grade requirements to be accepted into school. • What are the costs associated with playing at that level? What type of financial support do you have available to you?	November–June

Camps, combines, and provincial team tryouts: Start researching football camps and showcase and combine events you would like to attend during the summer. Things to look for when researching specific camps: coach involvement, camp type, cost, dates, time, and location.	April–May
Make your recruiting list: Begin to make a list of potential universities you would like to attend. When making your list, cast a wide net and look at as many universities and junior programs as possible. This way, you have more options. Make sure the school offers programs that interest you.	March–April
Attend as many online and in-person university and junior football seminars as possible. This will allow you to gain insight into the specific football program.	All year
Football and athletic development	
Participate in as many sports as possible, as they will build up your athletic abilities and limit the chances of overuse injuries.	All year
Attend as many performance camps as possible to develop your football skills. This is a great way to see how you measure up against players your age.	January–August
Play as many positions as possible on your team. It will allow you to learn the game faster, because you are playing the game from another perspective. It will also enable you to figure which position you like the most.	September–November
Join an organized strength and conditioning program or club.	January–August
Athletic treatment: Deal with any injuries that have occurred during the season. Taking care of your body is a part of being an athlete, and proper treatment and recovery allow you to perform at your best. **Hint:** To improve body movement and injury prevention, including fundamental mobility, adding stretching or yoga into your workouts will help.	All year
Exposure: Try out for the provincial and all-star teams, and attend showcase events to help boost your exposure.	January–July
Must do: Have a conversation with your head coach and position coach about things you can do to improve in your positional skill and as a football player.	August–September

GRADE 10 ACTION PLAN AND TO-DO CHECKLIST

Objectives

- Take care of your academics!
- Understand how the recruiting process works at Canadian universities, junior programs, and in the United States if you desire to play in the NCAA.
- Learn how to study. Developing good study habits early on will take you a long way.
- Figure out what direction you want to take to play football after high school.
- Understand the academic requirements and grade-point average expectations you need to be accepted into university and college. In addition, know what type of grades you require to receive an Athletic Financial Award at the U Sports level or obtain a Division I athletic scholarship.

Once you've decided that you want to play football after high school, you can now start working towards your goal. Since you still have a couple of years until graduation, you have some time, but there is a lot to do going forward, as time really does fly. The earlier you begin, the better your understanding of the recruiting process and how to navigate it, resulting in a greater success rate. For example, you should know the differences between official and unofficial campus visits. You should also understand what U Sports, NCAA, and junior coaches and recruiters want to know about you.

Grade 10 is the beginning stage of your journey as a student athlete. You will start to figure out your academic interests and begin to research what various universities or colleges offer academically. You will also want to research the different post-secondary football leagues from Canadian or American university football programs and non-academic junior football programs.

Even though it's early in the recruiting phase, it doesn't hurt to contact coaches to introduce yourself and express interest in playing for their program. As you are still in Grade 10, don't expect an instant response from coaches, because they tend to focus on the current recruiting class. This is okay, because you are still in the introductory phase as a potential student athlete recruit.

Starting early with the recruiting process allows coaches to know who you are earlier and identify you as a prospective recruit. In some unique cases, Canadian and American university football programs that really like a player and want them in their football program will present an offer as early as Grade 10.

However, something to consider is that your body matures between Grades 10 and 12, and you could be playing a different position in Grade 12 than you did in Grade 10. The goal is to research your football options, figure out what route you would like to take after graduation, and send film to coaches to begin introducing yourself.

These are the steps and tasks that *must* be taken to begin the recruiting process and help develop you into a complete student athlete.

COACH BURRIS INSIGHT:

Set a long-term goal and use short-term goals as checkpoints to ensure you are on the right track to achieve the long-term goal.

Grade 10 tasks and description	Time of year to execute
Personal	
Set your goals. Whether they are long- or short-term, start defining them. They will help you stay focused and measure how much progress you have or have not made. Suggested areas of focus when setting goals are academics, football, and personal.	July–August
Learn and develop time- and stress-management skills. Consult your head coach or guidance counsellor for strategies.	All year
Academics	
Develop a study routine. Learn when the best time for you to study is.	All year
Attend school and classes daily. Academics must be your priority at all times. **Hint:** Take advantage of tutorial times at school; typically, teachers are available to help students before and after school and at lunch.	September–June
Schedule an appointment with your guidance counsellor to set up a three-year plan with the goal of moving on to university. Meet at least once per semester or as necessary to ensure you are on the right academic track, as the goal is to attend university. Key questions to ask your guidance counsellor: • What are the *core classes* required to be accepted into university? • What score do I need to get on my SAT or ACT to play in the NCAA and obtain a full scholarship? • Where and how do I register to write the SAT? • Refer to page 20 in the NCAA Football section for SAT updates	September–June
If you have a realistic opportunity to play in the NCAA D1, D2, or D3, you must register with the NCAA Eligibility Center, which certifies you to be an NCAA student-athlete: www.ncca.com.	All year
Research	
Must do: Let your high school or community head coach and position coach know that you want to play post-secondary football. Your coaches can help provide recruiting insight and recommendations, and they can reach out to coaches at the next level.	
Must do: Stay current on important dates, U Sports blackout dates, admission application deadlines, and the NCAA recruiting calendar.	October–November

NCAA: If your goal is to play in the NCCA, look at the football testing numbers for different levels of the NCAA: NCAA D1, D2, or D3.	All year
Research and make a list of your top 15 Canadian universities, top 5 junior football teams, or—if the goal is to play NCAA football—the top 20 programs you are interested in attending. Your list should include the head coach and recruiting coordinator's contact information, including email and phone number.	January– August
Note: If your goal is to attend university, your research will also include looking up academic majors and program offerings at the university. The *USA Today* article "Ask your student these 20 questions to find his or her best college match" will help you with narrowing your decision: usatodayhss.com/2017/ask-your-studen t-these-20-questions-to-find-their-best-college-match	
Record the contact information so you have it when it's time to get in touch with the coaches. **Hint:** If there is a recruiting questionnaire on the team's website, fill it out.	January– August
Start analyzing team rosters of the universities or junior programs that interest you to gain insights. This will provide information on the measurable players at your position, player stats, how many players are at your position, and years of eligibility.	October– November
Highlight tape and exposure	
Make your highlight tape. Ensure that you have your best 10 to 15 plays at the beginning of your highlights, and be sure to identify yourself with an arrow or circle in the pre-snap. This will help coaches to find you before the ball is snapped. The goal is to keep the coaches' attention when they are reviewing your film. Email your highlight tape link to all the football programs of interest. Refer to Chapter 7: How to Make a Highlight Tape for more details. **Hint**: The best time to send your film is after your high school season.	October– November
Very important! Have a coach review your film before sending it out to football teams or posting on social media. Your coach can provide feedback about your highlight tape, such as if your clips are in the correct order or which clips to add or remove.	October– November

One of the best ways to gain exposure and interest from coaches is by using the Hudl platform. Post the finished copy of your highlight tape to all the major social media and sports platforms you are connected to. **Hint:** Make sure you have a Hudl account set up. Coaches are always looking for players on Hudl.	November
Football and athletic development	
Do not miss any team-training camp sessions, in-season practices, or team meetings.	August–November
Participate in as many sports as possible, as they will build your athletic abilities and limit the chances of injuries.	All year
Learn how to balance extracurricular activities and academics.	All year
Join an organized strength and conditioning program and positional skills program.	All year
You need to eat right if you want to see real gains from your strength and conditioning program. Finding a nutritionist is just as important as lifting weights.	January–February
Participate in as many football camps, elite team tryouts, and showcase events as possible. This will allow you to continue developing your football skills and gain exposure. **Hint:** Research local and out-of-town football combines and summer camps, and schedule the ones you would like to attend.	January–August
Athletic treatment: Deal with any injuries that have occurred during the season. Taking care of your body is part of being an athlete, and proper treatment and recovery allow you to perform at your best. **Hint:** To improve body movement and injury prevention, including fundamental mobility, adding stretching or yoga into your workouts will help.	All year
Rest: Schedule one to two weeks off to enjoy the summer. Recharge and have fun before school and the fall football season begins.	August
Optional	
Draft a cover letter to include with your highlight tape when sending to coaches.[4]	October–November

---

[4] Refer to or use our cover letter template in the Resource section.

THE BENEFITS OF SENDING OUT YOUR HIGHLIGHT FILM IN GRADE 10

- Coaches can identify and track your progress until you graduate from high school.
- It's an opportunity to gain feedback from coaches on what skills you need to improve.
- You might be invited to participate at their high school summer camp, which allows the coaches to see you in action.

If you follow the above action plan and to-do checklist, you will have had a productive Grade 10 year. Your foundation will be set up for success as a student athlete and, most importantly, you will have started the recruiting process. It is optional to follow up with coaches if you have not received any responses. Players can get a head start on recruiting in Grade 10, which will pay off down the road, but do not be discouraged if you do not receive much attention, as coaches tend to focus on the current recruiting class.

Now, let's get ready for Grade 11, the most important year academically, and for recruiting.

GRADE 11 ACTION PLAN AND TO-DO CHECKLIST

Objectives

1. Academics, academics, and academics. Your grades are critical in Grade 11. University coaches will ask you for your recent academic transcripts. They can determine if you are taking the correct courses and if you have the grades to get into school.
2. Register for your U Sports identification number.
3. If you plan on playing NCAA DI football, this is when you should write your SAT. If you do poorly on your first test, you have time to rewrite it before you graduate.
4. Gain exposure. Attend combines, performance camps, and summer camps. Try out for elite teams.

5. Contact coaches by phone or email, talk to them in person when you have the opportunity, and send them quality film. You should be ready to be recruited.

Your Grade 11 year is the most critical of the recruiting process. Since you are one year away from graduation, university and junior football coaches start to evaluate you more seriously. They want to learn more about you as a student, an athlete, and a person. If post-secondary coaches are interested in you, they will track your academic and football progress during your last two years of high school to ensure your eligibility.

Below are the steps and tasks that you must follow to develop into a complete student athlete, ready for recruitment.

Grade 11 tasks and description	Time of year to execute
Personal	
Revisit your Grade 10 goals and update them. Have you achieved them? As stated previously, your goals will help you stay focused and are a measuring stick to how much progress you have or have not made. Suggested areas of focus when setting goals are football, academics, and personal. These will help you to stay focused. **Hint:** Set a long-term goal and use short-term goals as checkpoints to ensure you are on the right track to achieve the long-term goal.	July–August
Continue to develop your time-management, study, and stress-management skills. If needed, consult your head coach or guidance counsellor for time-management and stress-management strategies.	All year
Register for your U Sports identification number. You will need this for on-campus visits and to register to play university football: usportscentral.ca/StudentCentre **Note:** There is a one-time fee of $50 when registering for your U Sports identification number, so be prepared.	All year
Rest. Schedule a week or two off to enjoy the summer. Recharge and have fun before school and the fall football season begins.	August
Academics	
Academics must be your priority. University coaches believe that if a student athlete has strong academics in Grade 11, the player will perform well academically in Grade 12. The numbers don't lie! Your Grade 11 academic performance is essential, as university coaches evaluate your marks as a measuring stick to see if you are academically healthy enough to get into university. • If you need help academically, seek it. Talk to coaches, guidance counsellors, or family members to get a tutor if needed. • **Hint:** Tutors cost money, but some YMCAs and libraries will have volunteer tutors. • Continue building solid study habits. • Take advantage of any resources that your high school may offer to improve your academic grades.	September–June

Meet with your guidance counsellor at least twice during the academic year or as needed to figure out if you are on the correct academic pathway to attend university or college. They will also provide information about university and college admissions, the application process, grade acceptance, and application deadlines. Find what you need to score on your SAT or ACT to play in the NCAA. Ask about the differences between the SAT and the ACT. SAT registration deadlines and SAT testing locations should be something you should ask about when meeting with your guidance counsellor. You will want to create a plan to write the test. If you are not interested in attending university, your guidance counsellor can provide you with other options or help make a career plan for life after graduation.	September–June
If you have a realistic opportunity to play in the NCAA DI, DII, or DIII, you must register with the NCAA Eligibility Center. Your registration certifies you as an NCAA student athlete. www.ncca.com	All year
SAT/ACT: Refer to page 20 in the NCAA Football section for SAT updates.	All year
Academic transcripts request: University and college coaches will ask for your Grade 11 academic transcripts. Have your most recent transcripts available, as coaches will need to review them to determine if you are taking the correct courses and eligible for admission. **Tip:** If you are an Alberta high school student and need access to your transcripts, you can order official transcripts or print unofficial transcripts at the myPass website: public.education.alberta.ca/PASI/mypass/welcome If this option is not available to you, talk to your guidance counsellor, principal, or football coach, and they will be able to point you in the right direction.	As soon as you receive your final grades

Research	
Must do: Have a conversation with your head coach and position coach about things you can do to improve your positional skill as a football player. You should now have an idea of which football direction you would like to pursue.	August–September
Must do: Stay current on important dates, U Sports blackout dates, admission application deadlines, and the NCAA recruiting calendar.	September
It's time to get specific on which football programs you are interested in and update your recruiting list. Decide on the top five teams you would like to play for at each level, and the top three for U Sports, NCAA and junior/CEGEP. Visit the websites of university/college and junior programs that you are interested in playing for. Make a list that includes the head coach and recruiting coordinator's email address, phone number, and football office contact if available. **Note:** If your goal is to attend university, your research will also include looking up academic programs offered at the university.	January–August
Record the contact information so you have it when it's time to email the coaches. If there is a recruiting questionnaire on the team's website, fill it out as well.	January–August
Highlight tape and exposure	
Make or update your highlight tape. Remember, you're selling yourself, so only add your best plays, be sure that your clips are clear, and you have indicated a pre-snap where you are on the field. **Hint:** Good-quality film goes a long way. Add your best 15 to 20 plays (no longer than three minutes of highlight clips), and include your best full game. Make sure your clips are not just ordinary plays. The best time to send a film is after your high school season. You can also send highlight clips of each game during the season. To learn how to put together your highlight tape, read Chapter 7: How to Make a Highlight Tape.	October–November
Have a coach review your highlight film before sharing.	October–November
Email your highlight tape to all of the football programs on your recruiting list. Your email should include your cover letter, highlight tape, and academic transcripts.	October–November

Post the finished copy of your highlight tape to all your social media, and share with teammates, family, friends and coaches. Most importantly, share your highlight tape with the post-secondary teams you are interested in playing for. The more you share your highlight tape, the more exposure you generate.	October–November
Football and athletic development	
Do not miss any team training camp sessions or in-season practices.	August–November
Participate in as many sports as possible to develop other skills and build your overall athleticism. This also limits the chances of injuries.	All year
Join an organized strength and conditioning program and positional skills program.	All year
Learn how to balance extracurricular activities and academics.	All year
Athletic treatment: Deal with any injuries that have occurred during the season. Taking care of your body is a part of being an athlete, and proper treatment and recovery enable you to perform at your best. **Hint:** To improve body movement and injury prevention, including fundamental mobility, adding stretching or yoga into your workouts will help.	All year
This is the year you start making a name for yourself. Participate in as many football camps, provincial team tryouts, and showcase events as possible. This will allow you to develop your football skills and gain exposure. Talk to as many coaches as possible on your exposure tour. The most important thing is that you are prepared to be recruited. **Hint:** Research local and out-of-town football combines and summer camps, and schedule the ones you would like to attend. **Hint:** If you made the U18 provincial team that participates in the Canada Cup tournament, you are now in a position to have all the universities in Canada looking at you play and practice for ten days. **Note:** Coaches can recruit you at the tournament, attracting recruiting interest if you perform well.	January–August

Optional	
Update your cover letter with any new football and academic accomplishments. The purpose of the cover letter is to introduce yourself to the coaches and let them know more about you. A well-written and short cover letter should include the following: • The year you will graduate • What academic program you would like to pursue in university • Any leadership and community service work you have done Ensure the letter is short and to the point, and that you have at least one coach as a reference, including their primary phone number and email address.	October–November
Coach's references: Ask your coach for a letter of reference that talks about you as a player and your character and leadership skills. If you are unable to get a reference letter, ask your coach if you can add their contact information, such as an email address and phone number.	October–November
Social media: Consider having a social media account that is strictly for football recruiting, and follow the coaches and teams that you are interested in playing for. This will help you stay up to date with the team. You can also directly send coaches your film through social media, which will help you get the edge as recruiting is very competitive. **Hint**: Use your professional name for your football account. Be sure to provide information such as height, weight, position, and graduation year on your profile.	All year

As mentioned before, Grade 11 will be your most important year during the recruiting process. Provided that you have excellent grades and you performed well during your season, coaches will have you on their recruiting list to sign you when you are in Grade 12. It's not uncommon for teams to sign players as early as Grade 11.

GRADE 12 ACTION PLAN AND TO-DO CHECKLIST

Congratulations! You are in your graduation year, and if you have been following our steps and action plan, you should have a good idea of the direction you will be heading post-graduation. This year you will decide which football program you will be taking your talents to. Enjoy the ride, you earned it. There will be more decisions to make this year due to the hype of signing day, graduation, and new beginnings. The best advice I can give you from experience and helping other players in your position is to enjoy this time, but stay focused on the task at hand and keep your foot on the gas pedal.

Objectives

- Graduate with good grades that will get you into university. This also applies to players who do not want to attend university. You never know, down the road you may want to go to university, so you will have to have the grades to do so.
- Have a great season. Be your best as a player and a teammate. Have fun!
- Confirm which direction you want to take football if you're still undecided.
- Go on official campus visits or attend CJFL spring camps.
- Commit and sign to the program that fits you best.
- Enjoy the moment and the experience—the high school recruiting process only happens once.

If you're still undecided in which football direction you are heading, make your choice. You will need to continue sending out your player package. The biggest thing is that you do not want any programs to forget about you. Staying proactive is vital during the recruiting process. Update your football cover letter and résumé, and add your most recent awards and accomplishments.

Grade 12 tasks and description	Time of year to execute
Personal	
Remember, goal-setting is a measuring stick of your commitment and progress towards your goal. Revisit your Grade 11 goals. Did you achieve them? Your goals will be different now, as you will be transitioning away from high school. They should be more specific and detailed, so revise and set new goals for football, academics, personal development, and post-graduation. Continue to develop time-management and stress-management skills. **Hint:** Set a long-term goal, and use short-term goals as checkpoints to ensure you are on the right track to achieve the long-term goal.	July–August
Register for your U Sports identification number. Take action *now* if you have not already done so. You need the U Sports identification number to go on an official Canadian university campus visit and play Canadian university football. To register for the U Sports number, follow this link: usportscentral.ca/ StudentCentre **Note:** there is a one-time fee of $50 associated when registering, so prepare accordingly.	September
NCAA Eligibility Center: Players must be certified by the NCAA Eligibility Center to play NCAA Division I or II football: www.ncaa.org	September
Rest: Schedule a week or two off to enjoy the summer. Recharge and have fun before school and the fall football season begins.	August

Academics	
Academics is always number one. Continue working to be the best student you can and work hard to achieve good grades. By the second semester, you will know if you have been accepted to a university or college if you decide to go that route. **Note:** Even if your goal is not to go to university or college, your mindset should be the same as a student who wants to attend university: work to achieve the best grades possible. **Hint:** Tutors cost money, but some YMCAs and libraries have volunteer tutors.	September–June
Guidance and support: Your high school guidance counsellor will play a more significant role as this is your graduation year. There are various ways they can help, such as completing your admission applications and finding and applying to bursaries to help with university or college tuition. If post-secondary education is not of interest, guidance counsellors will help you map out your future for life after high school. **Tip:** Be sure to discuss university application deadlines. You want to make sure you meet the application deadlines of the school you are interested in. Your guidance counsellor will help you with this process. **Hint:** If your grades are questionable for university admission, you have some options. You can upgrade by taking summer classes, or you can play a year of junior football out of high school and upgrade your academics.	September–June
SAT/ACT: If your goal is to play in the NCAA please refer to page 20 in the NCAA Football section for SAT updates.	September–February
Academic transcripts request: Have your most recent academic transcripts available. Coaches will need to review your transcripts to determine if you are taking the correct courses to be eligible for university acceptance. **Hint:** If you are an Alberta high school student and need access to your transcripts, you can order official transcripts or print unofficial transcripts at the myPass website: public.education.alberta.ca/PASI/mypass/welcome Or talk to your guidance counsellors, principal, or football coach, and they will be able to point you in the right direction.	February–May

Research	
If you've been following the steps in this book, you should know which football path you will be taking once you graduate from high school. You will have narrowed down the football programs you are considering, and at which level. Your research is not complete! A couple of questions to ask yourself: • Have you explored all your football options after high school? • Have you taken all your official campus visits if offered? • Have you met all the academic requirements to get into school?	February–May
If you are late to the recruiting process, there is work to be done. Make a recruiting list of your top five university or junior programs and visit their websites. Your list should include the head coach and recruiting coordinators' email address, phone number, and football office contact if available. **Note:** If your goal is to attend university, your research will also include looking up academic programs and majors offered at the university. Be sure that the schools of interest have the program you are interested in. **Never base your decision on the football program alone.**	September–November
Record the contact information so you have it when it's time to email the coaches. If there is a recruiting questionnaire on the team's website, fill it out as well.	September–November

Highlight tape and exposure	
Grade 12 highlight tape: Combine your best clips from all the high school seasons. This will allow coaches to see your body of work. Remember, you are selling yourself and your talent. Be sure to add your best plays, and make sure you indicate a pre-snap in which you are located on the field. **Hint:** Good quality film goes a long way. Add your best 15 plays (no longer than three minutes of highlight clips) and include your best full game. **Hint:** Make sure your clips are not just ordinary plays. The best time to send the film would be after your high school season. To learn how to put together your highlight tape, read Chapter 7: How to Make a Highlight Tape.	October–November
Have a coach review your highlight film before sending it out.	October
By now, you should have a good idea of which direction you are heading and which football program has an interest in you. Send your highlight tapes to all the specific football programs you are interested in that have interest in you.	October–November
Post the finished copy of your highlight tape to all your social media and sports platforms.	October–November
Football and athletic development	
Do not miss any team training camp sessions, in-season practices, or team meetings.	August–November
Participate in as many sports as possible to develop other athletic skills to build your overall athleticism and limit the chances of overuse injuries.	All year
Learn how to balance extracurricular activities and academics.	All year
Get in the best shape of your life by joining an organized strength and conditioning program and positional-skills program. Remember, you are now preparing to compete for a higher competition level.	September–June
Participate in as many winter and spring football camps and showcase events as possible. This will allow you to gain additional exposure. This stage is especially relevant if you are still unsigned or late to the recruiting process.	December–March

Athletic treatment: Deal with any injuries that have occurred during the season. Taking care of your body is a part of being an athlete, and proper treatment and recovery allow you to perform at your best. **Hint:** To improve body movement and injury prevention, including fundamental mobility, adding stretching or yoga in your with your workouts will help.	All year
Decisions and transitional phase	
Canadian University or NCAA: Take official campus visits if they are offered by the university.	January–June
Confirm that you have been accepted to university.	March
Decide and commit to which university program you will be attending.	February–May
If you decide to play junior football, attend the specific junior team's spring camp.	April–May
On June 1, CJFL signing day, decide which program fits you best.	June
Optional	
Update your cover letter and résumé with any new football and academic accomplishments. The purpose of the cover letter is to introduce yourself to the coaches and let them know more about you. **Hint:** You do not want your letter to be too long, but make sure you are as detailed as possible. A well-written cover letter should include the following: • The year you will graduate • What academic program you would like to pursue in university • Any leadership and community service work you have done	October–November
Coach's references: Ask your coach for a letter of reference that speaks to who you are as a player and your character and leadership skills. If you are unable to get a reference letter, ask your coach if you can add their contact information, such as an email address and phone number.	October–November

By the end of your Grade 12 year, one of two things should happen: you have signed and committed to a post-secondary program, or you have a clear plan for your next step in transitioning out of high school.

CHAPTER 5

What Recruiting Coordinators Look for in High School Recruits

In this chapter, we will go over each position and list the skills recruiters look for. This list comes from multiple coaches across Canada at the university and junior levels. When coaches and recruiters evaluate players, they look to see what specific skill set you have. If you're in Grade 9 or 10, you have the opportunity to learn what post-secondary coaches are looking for in each position and skill set. This will give you an edge, because you can start working on the positional skills and apply them to your game.

In order to build a winning football program, recruiters and coaches at the post-secondary level must bring in players who can develop within the team and have leadership skills. They need the best athletes, those who are skilled and who will consistently work hard. Recruiters are also looking for that rare athlete who has tremendous muscular size, height and weight, combined with speed, strength, and skill.

They are seeking players who fit the culture of their specific football program.

> *When I talk to recruits on the phone, I want them to know what types of coverages they are playing at their high school and be able to talk about it. I can tell when kids are just saying cliché things they think coaches want to hear, so I try and ask about the specifics of what they are doing.*

Brandon Dubs, U Sports
Special Teams Coordinator/ Defensive Backs Coach

Understand that coaches do not want players who only demonstrate tremendous athletic ability, they want athletes who have skills and smarts too. Below, we'll take a look at what attributes recruiters are looking for in each position.

QUARTERBACKS

Photo credit: Eclectic Shots Photography

- The quarterback must be a good decision maker and be able to think and throw.
- Quarterback-specific footwork on run plays and pass plays: rollouts, play-action, 1-step, 3-step, 5-step rhythm drops
- The quarterback must be able to go through their reads progressions and recognize defensive coverages
- Quarterbacks must have the following skill set: leadership, effective communication, a strong work ethic, competitiveness, and consistency
- Athleticism and balance

- Solid pocket present and escape ability to avoid the pass-rush pressure on their interior and back sides
- Quarterback passing skills: accuracy, can throw all route-tree passes, can get the ball to pass catchers efficiently
- Centre and quarterback changes and quarterback and running back exchanges
- Field vision: the ability to scan the field and identify the open recovers
- Ball-handling skills: the ability to catch shotgun snaps and under-centre snaps, as well as exchanges with the running backs

OFFENSIVE LINE

Photo credit: Piper Sports Photography

OFFENSIVE CENTRE

- Must be able to get into the correct stance, and the offensive linemen must be able to explode out of their stance
- Toughness
- Good decision-making, awareness, and understanding of defensive front and schemes

- Body quickness and first- and second-step quickness
- Size, athleticism, flexibility, balance, strength, and explosiveness
- Long snaps when the quarterback is in shotgun
- Run blocking, blocking with power, maintaining a low pad level, and accurate hand placement; the ability to remove players by dipping hips and striking with power and running your feet; double team effectiveness
- Pass protection, footwork, ability to handle power moves from a defensive lineman. The ability to punch and anchor is an important skill an offensive linemen must develop to play at a high level
- The centre must be able to pull and trap, and have good technique when attacking defensive linemen.
- The ability to play physically and finish blocks
- The ability to play mean and with tenacity
- The ability to punch and strike with power

OFFENSIVE GUARDS

- Must be able to get into the correct stance, and the offensive linemen must be able to explode out of their stance
- Stance flexibility: must bend at the hips, knees, and ankles
- Toughness
- Size, athleticism, quickness, strength, and balance
- How well you get to the second level (linebackers) and open-field blocking
- Run blocking, block with power, pad level, and hand placement; ability to remove players; double teams' effectiveness
- Pass protection, footwork, and the ability to handle power moves from a defensive lineman
- Good footwork and agility in both open and tight spaces
- Sound pulling and trap technique
- The ability to play physically and finish blocks

- The ability to play mean and with tenacity
- The ability to punch and strike with power is an important skill an offensive linemen must develop to play at a high level

OFFENSIVE TACKLES

- Must be able to get into the correct stance, and the can the offensive linemen must be able to explode out of their stance
- Stance flexibility: must bend at the hips, knees, and ankles
- Toughness
- Size, athleticism, quickness, strength, and balance
- Run-blocking skills: block with power, maintain a low pad level, and have good hand placement
- Pass protection, footwork, and being able to handle power moves from a defensive lineman
- Pass protection; being able to use footwork and quickness to play in one-on-one situations
- Open-field blocking
- Sound pulling and trap technique
- Must have the ability to play physically and finish blocks, as well as play mean and with tenacity
- The ability to effectively punch and strike with power

RUNNING BACKS AND FULLBACKS

Photo credit: Connie Nichol

RUNNING BACKS

- Ball security skills
- Run instincts and vision
- Athleticism, power, balance, speed, and explosiveness
- Run/pass blocking skills and effort blocking skills
- Receiving skills: you must be able to catch the football with your hands instead of your body
- Rushing skills: the ability to run inside and outside of offensive tackles
- The ability to play with power, speed, and finesse
- Can gain yards after contact

- Tackle avoidance skills
- Durability

FULLBACKS

- Excellent run-blocking skills, and the ability to block with power and move defenders
- Rushing skills: must be able to create your own yards, especially on short yardage situations
- The ability to run inside in between the tackles; must be tough to bring down
- Can gain yards after contact
- Excellent pass-protection skills
- The ability to play with toughness, explosiveness, and durability
- Receiving skills: you must be able to catch the football with your hands instead of only catching the football your body.
- Good offensive intelligence

RECEIVERS AND PASS CATCHERS

- Speed, explosiveness and the ability to separate from the defender
- Body control and athleticism
- Protecting the football (ball security)
- Run-blocking skills: ability to break down with a low pad level and violently strike the defender, run feet to move the player out of the running path
- Downfield blocking skills
- Catching skills: must have the ability to catch the ball with hands rather than your body. What is your catching radius like? Can you catch in coverage? Can the receiver make contested catches?
- Must be able to efficiently run all of the passing routes
- Release technique skills
- Can gain yards after contact; tackle avoidance
- Field awareness and the ability to recognize defensive coverage
- Ability to play special teams

DEFENSIVE LINE

Photo credit: Connie Nichol

DEFENSIVE ENDS

- Must have a great stance to burst out of when the ball is snapped
- Speed and quickness, explosiveness, superior quick-twitch
- Physical skill: explosiveness, strength, and power
- Athleticism, flexibility, bend, read, and reaction skills
- Run-stopping technique and skill; must be able to play the run
- Pass-rush skills and counter skills
- Tackling and turnover skills
- Awareness and quarterback-contain skills
- Hand use and the ability to defeat, get off block, and effectively strike
- Awareness and instinct
- Football IQ

DEFENSIVE TACKLES

- Must have a great stance to burst out of when the ball is snapped
- Quickness and explosiveness
- Strength and power
- Athleticism, flexibility, strength, read, and reaction skills
- Leverage and power. Defensive tackles must be able to play lower than the offensive linemen and bull rush. Must be able to play the run
- Run-stopping technique and skill: how well can the defensive linemen reset the line of scrimmage? Can he play with extension and low pad level versus the run? Can the player take on and defeat double-teams?
- Pass rush and hand skills: how well can the player clear, replace, and control hands? Must be able to use counter moves effectively.
- Tackling and turnover skills
- Hand use and the ability to defeat and get off block and effectively strike
- Relentless effort and pursuit
- Football IQ, awareness, and instinct

LINEBACKERS

Photo credit: Don Martin

- Good leadership skills
- Excellent tackling skills: wrapping up and finishing tackles, taking correct angles, and attacking tackles
- Run and pass footwork, vision, and reaction skills
- Athleticism, size, and speed
- Pass-coverage skills
- Blitzing skills
- Awareness and ball skills: knockdowns, interceptions, and strips
- Relentless effort and pursuit

DEFENSIVE BACKS

Photo credit: Connie Nichol

HALFBACKS

- Footwork: must have good backpedal and acceleration skills
- Loose, fluid, and swiveling hips for changing direction
- Transition: how does the athlete break and flip his hips? Is the athlete's transition from movement to movement smooth or choppy?
- Blitzing skills
- Tackling skills: open-field tackling and tackling to support the run
- Coverage skills: man-to-man and zone coverage
- Ability to track the ball in the air, make good ball judgment, and attack and break to the ball
- Relentless effort and pursuit
- Ball skills: high-pointing the ball, catching, turnover skills

CORNERBACKS

- Self-confidence: play man coverage without support; self-confidence needed
- Footwork and backpedal skills, breaking and attacking the football
- Transition: how does the athlete break and flip his hips? Is the transition from movement to movement smooth or choppy?
- Excellent football intelligence
- Loose, fluid, and swiveling hips for changing direction
- Coverage skills: man-to-man and zone coverage skills
- Jam receivers accurately
- Tackling to support the run
- Good body control and positioning
- Ball skills: high-pointing the ball, catching, and turnover skills
- Can track the ball in the air and make good ball judgment

FREE SAFETY

- Self-confidence
- Excellent football intelligence; must understand route combinations, down and distance tendencies, and have the ability to react to route based on alignment and film study
- Transition: how does the athlete break and flip his hips? Is the athlete's transition from movement to movement smooth or choppy?
- Footwork: backpedal and breaking to the ball
- Loose, fluid, and swiveling hips for changing direction
- Open-field tackling skills and tackling skills to support the run
- Open-field speed to close on the football
- Range: ability to cover all ground
- Ball skills: high-pointing the ball, catching the ball, and turnover skills
- Coverage skills: man-to-man and zone coverage skills
- Ability to track the ball in the air and make good ball judgment

SPECIALISTS

Photo credit: Eclectic Shots Photography

PUNTER

- Punt accuracy and placement
- Hang time before the ball descends
- Ability to handle bad snaps
- Power: how far can the player punt? 45-yards-plus is considered elite.
- Athleticism: can the player execute fake punts?
- Must be able to catch the football from the long snapper
- Ability to make tackles if needed

KICKER

- Self-confidence
- Consistency with kicking successful field goals and kickoffs

- Range: how far can the player make field goals? 15 to 50 yards.
- Positive field-goal-per-attempt percentage
- Athletic ability
- Kick-off skills: placement, distance, and short kick
- Onside kick skills
- Power: how far can the player kick a field goal?

KICK, PUNT, AND FIELD GOAL RETURNERS

- Superior hands to catch punts and secure the football
- Always positive yards gained; provide positive field position
- Vision and speed
- Tackle avoidance
- Tremendous concentration

BODY TYPE

There are post-secondary football programs at the U Sports and NCAA levels that have positional charts that outline specific body-type measurable ranges they want their recruits to fall into. For example, some teams might only recruit wide receivers who are 6 foot 3, 200 pounds, and run 4.3 40-yard dash times. At the U Sports level, a player's body-type measurables are not as strict as in the NCCA; talent and performance productivity are taken into consideration more than specific measurables.

A player who doesn't meet the "eyeball test" and is considered undersized shouldn't be discouraged.[5] You have no control over which body you were given. Instead, you should focus on what you can control, which is skill, speed, strength, and overall athleticism. If you can be among the top in what you can control and make plays, you put yourself in a position to help your team win games. Canadian coaches *will* recruit players who do not meet the eyeball test.

---

[5] See glossary for the definition of "eyeball test."

CHAPTER 6

Making a Recruiting List

Making your recruiting list doesn't have to be complicated. This is a great opportunity to research specific Canadian and American universities and junior and CEGEP football programs so you can make an informed decision when it's time to decide which school you would like to attend as a student athlete.

Your recruiting list will help you target the right school and football program for you.

---

1. Make a list of the top 10 universities and junior programs you would like to attend. Complete this list in Grade 11.

1.	6.
2.	7.
3.	8.
4.	9.
5.	10.

2. Five things to think about when making your list and doing the research:

Does the school have the program you are interested in?

What are the costs involved to attend school if going to university or CEGEP?

What is the cost involved in playing junior football, if that's the pathway you're taking?

Do you want to attend a school in a big city or a small town? Where is the school located?

Would you attend this university if you were not playing football?

What are the academic requirements?

Athletically, does your football skill set and athleticism match the football program?

What does the team depth chart look like? You don't want to go to a school that is overloaded with players who play your position.

3. Rank the university, junior and/or CEGEP programs, from the ones that are the best fit for you academically and athletically to the ones that might be competitive, where playtime might be *limited*, or where you might receive no playtime in your freshmen and sophomore year. Complete this list right after your Grade 12 football season, when recruiting really picks up.

Best fit	Limited
1.	1.
2.	2.
3.	3.
4.	4.
5.	5.
6.	6.

Your recruiting list will change every year as your interests and goals change—that's completely normal. Frequently revise and update your list. This will help you to stay organized to make your decision in Grade 12.

CHAPTER 7
How to Make a Highlight Tape

Your highlight tape is what sells you as a football player, and it's one of the most effective tools for coaches. Besides letting coaches see you play live, film also allows them to see you perform up close and personal. So, having high-quality highlight film with the correct angles goes a long way. Presenting a sharp highlight tape can be the reason coaches become interested in you.

Ultimately, your football performance is what makes coaches watch your whole film; if your highlight tape is poorly edited or has a lack of explosive plays, coaches will stop watching. When making your highlight tape, be sure to showcase your full athletic ability. For example, if you're a defensive player, you want to show your tackling, change-of-direction, and coverage skills, your drop into coverage, speed and pursuit, and the ability to track down offensive players. Coaches also want to see plays where you give unusual effort and a relentless finish.

STEPS TO MAKING YOUR HIGHLIGHT TAPE

Below are some tips for making your highlight tape. It should be two to three minutes max of your best plays. Also, include your two best full games. Coaches want to evaluate your talent fully, so providing a full game or your best half game will assist in their assessment of you.

COACH BURRIS INSIGHT:

Before you start making your highlight tape, understand that there are hundreds of players following the same process for theirs. This tip will help you to stand out:

Personalize and customize the video introduction to each program for which you're applying. Select your top five to ten schools of interest and tailor the introduction as necessary.

This is an extra step, but you will see better results. Of course, this will not guarantee that you will be recruited or offered an Athletic Financial Award or full scholarship, but it will help you stand out from the rest, and you will have a better chance of receiving a response from the coaches.

Below is an example of a short script that you can use to create a personalized video introduction to send to coaches attached to your highlight tape. Feel free to use it or come up with your own.

Hey, Coach.

My name is Jackson Fresh. I am a 6 foot 5, 290-pound defensive lineman from Scarborough, Ontario. I wanted to let you know that I am very interested in playing football in the Atlantic University Sports Conference for the Huskies. It has been a long-time dream of mine to play for the Huskies. I would love to attend camp or have the opportunity to get to know you and your assistant coaches in the near future. I have attached my highlight recruiting tape, which you can watch on this video. Thank you for your time.

INFORMATION TO INCORPORATE

Every highlight tape should start with the following information, or it should be in the bio section:	
First and last name:	Jackson Fresh
Position:	DL/OL
Height and weight:	6'5", 280 pounds
Contact information **Phone number:** **Email:**	403-111-1111 J.Fresh@mail.com
High school name and location:	Cedarbrae Collegiate Institute Scarborough, Ontario
Head coach name: **Contact info:**	Coach Victory, Head Coach, Cedarbrae Colts Football Direct: 403-333-3333, Ext. 2000; email: victory@cci.ca

CLIPS TO INCLUDE

Find the best 15 to 20 plays of your season and include your best full game.	☐
Be sure that each clip's footage is clear and that you can be clearly identified.	☐
If you are in Grade 12, you can add your best plays from your previous high school seasons as well.	☐
Be sure to organize your clips, starting with your best.	☐
When making your highlight tape, be sure to show all your skill sets, such as: • long snapping • field goal kicking • punting • kick returns • punt returns Coaches also want to see you compete, and your effort level. If you have plays that show high effort, add them to your film.	☐ ☐ ☐ ☐ ☐ ☐
Additional notes:	

MULTIPLE POSITIONS

If you play multiple positions, organize your highlight clips accordingly. For example, if you play running back and linebacker, you want to have all your running back plays together, with all your best ones at the beginning. Then, organize all your linebacker plays together, starting with the best ones. Be sure to include a screenshot that communicates your position with your jersey number and colour. Make it easy on the coaches and provide as many details as possible.

PRE-SNAP INDICATOR

Now that you have your clips in place, it's time to add your pre-snap indicator. It is strongly recommended that you add an arrow, circle, or a star to show where you are before the snap. Make it easy for coaches to find you on your film. The less work they have to do to find you, the more attention they will have on your football skill.

MUSIC

If you decide you want to add music to your highlight tape, be sure that the language is appropriate or that it's a clean version of a song. A lot of college coaches watch highlight film on mute. The coaches' sole priority is evaluating the film and finding out if the players fit their program. If you decide to add music, my recommendation is to use edited music to prevent inappropriate language or instrumentals. Or you can simply make two copies of your highlight tape, a clean copy for coaches and another as a personal copy.

SHARING YOUR FILM

Before posting and sharing your highlight tape, have your coach review it to make sure your clips are arranged correctly, and your best plays are front-loaded. Be sure your highlights are clips that show maximum effort, making standout plays. This will help keep the coaches' attention.

Once your film is ready, you will want to share and post it *everywhere*. Post and tag your highlight tape on all social media platforms. Share and tag it with coaches, teammates, family, and friends. Add your highlight tape link on all your social media profile bios, so it's visible and easy for coaches to see if they come across your page. Tag and direct-message your highlight tape link to coaches and recruiting coordinators.

VIDEO ANGLES

Be sure to use the correct video angle. It is best to use a tight/end zone angle for linemen. The tight angle provides the best view to see linemen in action. For the skilled positions, using wide-angle video is the best practice. Below are the photos of each angle. If you cannot get these specific video angles, use the best film you have access to.

TIGHT ANGLE/END-ZONE ANGLE FOR LINEMEN

The angle in the photo below is called "tight/end zone angle." If you are a lineman, this is the angle you should use when making your highlight tape. This provides the best view for coaches to see and evaluate your skill and technique.

Note: Most of the film that university and college programs receive in Canada is from the wide angle. So, linemen, if your football program only films the wide angle, don't worry. Coaches can still evaluate your film. They can see how well you get off the ball, your pad level, and your aggression effort to get the ball. Coaches will struggle to see your technique, however.

WIDE ANGLE FOR SKILLED POSITIONS

The wide angle is specifically for the skilled non-linemen positions, because it covers the whole field and you can see the entire play develop from start to finish. The wide angle is the most popular one used when filming all positions, but it's more specific to the skilled positions.

COACH BURRIS INSIGHT:

If you cannot get these specific angles or the high-definition quality in the photos, just use the best available film you have access to.

COMMON MISTAKES

It is always an exciting time when making your highlight tape for recruiting purposes and showing the world your talents. However, there are some common mistakes, outlined below:

Circle yes or no if any of the following apply to your film:	
Is your highlight tape too long?	yes/no
Are you adding ordinary, everyday plays?	yes/no
Are you front-loading the tape with the best plays? *Most coaches will not watch more than one to two minutes of your highlight tape.*	yes/no
Are you highlighting yourself before the ball is snapped in the play?	yes/no
Have you ensured the music you added has clean language? *Make duplicates of your highlight tape and send the clean copy to the coaches.*	yes/no
If showing multiple position highlights, are they organized in order of position?	yes/no
Have you added vital information at the beginning of the highlight tape, such as full name, position(s), and contact information?	yes/no
Have you asked your coach to review your finished highlight tape to ensure it's done correctly and your plays are in the correct order? *Any feedback about your tape can help improve the quality of your film.*	yes/no
Additional notes:	

Recruiting does not require a lot of game film. In fact, coaches want to see quality film that shows good technique and explosive effort over many ordinary plays. So, if you have fifteen highlight clips that show relentless effort and explosive plays, those are what you're going to want to highlight. For example, if you're a running back and you have a 40-yard touchdown run, and you break five tackles on that run, that is what coaches want to see. Fifteen explosive plays are better than thirty regular plays.

SOCIAL MEDIA

Post-secondary coaches are now looking at personal social media pages to gain insight into who you are. It goes without saying that your social media pages do not contain problematic content such as racism, discrimination against women, or demeaning or violent acts. Such a player will not succeed in this community. It will raise red flags to coaches about what type of person you are. Remember, coaches are looking for the best student athletes who fit their football program's culture; it's not just about who the best football player is.

Next, be sure to follow the coaches and the football programs that you are interested in attending. Then you want to post impressive clips of you making plays on the football field, your personal best in the weight room, running your 40-yard dash, or even doing impressive athletic feats that are not football-related. Coaches love to see how athletic you are, and it keeps them solely focused on you.

The best social media platform for reaching out to U Sports and NCAA football coaches is Twitter. It's the easiest way to find coaches. Follow them and send direct messages to them this way.

Also, remember that NCAA teams are restricted from contacting you directly until you begin Grade 11. Then players will be able to receive text messages, direct messages on social media platforms, and emails from coaches. This is part of the NCAA recruiting rules.

CHAPTER 8

Visiting Campuses

It is time to take your official campus visit. Let's get you into the right mindset so you can see past the smoke. The purpose of the campus visit is to tell you more about the school's football program and facilities, and show you around the campus. Every program is different in how it organizes its visits, so expect to have other recruits with you.

If a university program is bringing you in, know that they are serious about you becoming a student athlete with their program. The coaches and their players will do their best to make your visit perfect and sell you on committing to their program.

You have the recruiting leverage and are in the driver's seat. Regardless of how good a time they show you on your visit, your decision ultimately comes down to your future goals. You do not want to go to a school that doesn't have the academic program you want to pursue.

COACH BURRIS INSIGHT:

When a head coach, assistant coach, athletic director, athletic trainer, or academic advisor presents information, put your cellphone away. Unless you're taking a photo, give the speaker or coach your undivided attention. Also, ensure you're clean and dress appropriately for the occasion. You will want to make a strong impression on the coaches. Make sure you introduce yourself to all the coaches if you have the opportunity. Making eye contact, smiling, and a having a firm handshake will help your introduction to the coaches.

QUESTIONS TO ASK

Go on your visits with a list of questions prepared for the coaches. Take advantage of this opportunity and talk to the players on the team. They will provide you with insight into the team culture and their personal experiences as university student athletes. The more information you know about the university and the football program, the easier it will be to make an informed decision.

The visit will be fast-paced, and a lot of information will be thrown at you. It will be difficult to absorb everything all at once, so be sure to ask a lot of questions and enjoy the experience when you're on your visit.

Whether you are planning on playing junior or university football, you need to have questions prepared for the head coach or the team recruiter. Do your research on the university and the football program prior to the phone call or campus visit. Coaches love it when players have questions prepared. It shows initiative and that you're mature and interested in their program.

You should consider any conversation with coaches or team recruiters a causal interview. They will ask a lot of questions about football, your education, and even your family. Do not be afraid to ask the following questions during a phone conversation, on a campus visit, or during spring camp. This list contains 21 questions; feel free to add more and write down the answers you receive from coaches. I would recommend reviewing these questions before any conversations or visits with post-secondary coaches.

COACH BURRIS INSIGHT:

Positional coaches: Teams who have two to three coaches at one position normally have a strong positional unit, and each player will receive ample attention and coaching to accelerate their positional development.

What are the priority positions you will be looking at in my recruiting class?

Can you outline how the recruiting process works for your program?

What is a typical day like for athletes in- and off-season?

What are the academic expectations of the players?

Do freshmen have the chance to come in and compete for playing time?

Is there any academic support in- and off-season?

What is your team philosophy and coaching style?

What do most players do for living arrangements?

Who is the position coach, and what are they like?

What is the playbook like? Is it complex to learn?

What's the athletic offer?

Am I eligible to receive an athletic award?

Are there part-time jobs available during the off-season?

Does the university have an alumni support program in place post-graduation?

How many positional coaches are there for my position?

Does your program provide strategic course scheduling assistance?

Who are the strength coaches, and how do the in- and off-season strength and conditioning programs work?

What is the player depth like for my position?

What should I consider when seeking accommodations? Is it recommended to live on or off campus?

What type of course load do you suggest I take in and out of season?

Which position are you recruiting me to play for in your program?

Additional Questions

COACH BURRIS INSIGHT:

Strategic course schedule assistance is when the academics advisor or one of the coaches helps you select your classes, dates, and times. This was a major help to me in my first year of university, because the coaches or academic advisors know the flow of the season and when and when not to schedule classes. There are multiple ways to customize your classes, depending on what type of student you are. For example, if course times are available, you can schedule all your classes in the morning, or have two days with a heavy course load. It depends on what type of student you are, and this will play a big role in setting up your academic schedule.

COACH BURRIS INSIGHT:

Players and parents must understand that being accepted into a university in Canada doesn't mean you automatically qualify for an Athletic Financial Award. The players still need to meet specific academic requirements. Each athletic conference has unique demands. Be sure to do the research to find out if you qualify.

QUESTIONS TO AVOID ASKING

Before you go on your official campus visit, you will want to research the university and the football program to learn as much as possible so you can go on the visit prepared. Think about it this way: university coaches and recruiters have done their research on you, and they expect you to do your research on their school and football program.

If you go into your visit asking the questions below, it's a red flag to the coaches that you might not be interested in their program because you didn't do your research.

You can find the answers to these questions below with an internet search. The goal is to make a good impression on the coaching staff and learn as much as possible about the university and football program so you can make an informed decision about which program to choose, so avoid asking the following questions:

- What was the team's record last season?
- Does the university have my academic program?
- What conference does the team play in?
- Why do you need to talk to my high school coach?
- When will you be making an offer?
- Will I dress every game, and will I be a starter in my first year?

MAKING THE BIG DECISION

You should not make this decision based only on football. It's not a five-year decision; it's a forty-year decision, meaning this moment and opportunity should be a springboard to setting you up for life after football.

What a time to be alive as a student athlete recruit! The smoke is clearing, and by Grade 12 you should have a clearer picture of which program has an interest in you and which you would like to commit to. One of the hardest decisions to make during the recruiting process is which program to choose. It's about more than football, so these are things you should consider when making your decision.

GETTING WHAT YOU WANT

When deciding which university to attend, you have to be specific about what you want. For example, you may choose to go to a smaller university in a small town that has small class sizes and the academic program you're interested in. Many players have made big mistakes by deciding to go to a university based solely on the football program's success and not on their personal preference, and they have regretted it.

To ensure you're making the right decision, answer the following questions honestly:

What's is the cost of tuition?

How much debt will you accumulate while playing football?

What does the school have to offer academically, and what is the academic reputation of the university? Are you comfortable with the learning environment at the school?

Do you like the city or town where the football program is located? Do you want to live close to home or far away? Do you want to live in the city or a small college town?

Do you prefer living in the city or small town for four years or more? If you were to get hurt and couldn't play for the season, would you still like living in the city or town?

Did you like the head coach's, positional coach's, and team's philosophies?

Did you like the team culture?

What offensive, defensive, and special team systems does the team run? Does your football skill set fit in with the team's system?

What is the athletic treatment (physio) like?

COACH BURRIS INSIGHT:

The most underrated factors when deciding on a program: does the university have any alumni support programs in place for post-graduation? Are there any internships available after graduation, if going to university?

CHAPTER 9

Signing the Letter of Intent—Now What?

Once you have signed the letter of intent, you are agreeing to becoming a student athlete at that university. Congratulations on this big accomplishment! Now it's time for you to flip your mindset and prepare to be a student athlete at the university level. How you approach your preparation *must* be different than high school. For example, you now have to train and study like a university student, and master your craft as a football player, which means mastering your positional skills. Your accomplishments in high school no longer matter once you get to university or junior football. Your new teammates were great players at the high school level as well. You will have to start all over again to compete and prove yourself to the coaching staff and your teammates.

Now that you signed and committed to a football program, it's time to move on and prepare for the next phase of entering your university or junior/CEGEP team. Regardless of whether you are playing at the junior/CEGEP or university level, the environment is competitive, and you will be competing with teammates in the weight room and for playing time, not to mention competing against yourself to achieve the highest academic grades possible.

COACH BURRIS INSIGHT:

Your job is to go training camp, compete, and make the veteran players in your position feel uncomfortable, and apply pressure because you are competing at a high level and looking to move up the depth chart and earn playing time. In order to do this, you must have a full understanding of the playbook, grit, and a competitive edge that comes from within to find success at the next level.

PLAYBOOK, TIME MANAGEMENT, AND INDEPENDENT LEARNING

Here are a few important steps that may not have crossed your mind yet, or that were placed on to the back burner during the recruiting process. Go through this list and check off the task and date when completed. It is important that you complete all tasks in order so you can be at your best and most prepared heading to your new team.

Important considerations		Date completed
Finish high school academically strong.	☐	
Make sure you have been accepted to the university you decided to attend.	☐	
Complete any outstanding paperwork required for school or the football team.	☐	
Research any government scholarships or bursaries that might be available.	☐	
Build a living-expenses budget. This is important to help manage and understand where your money is going. Build a budget with your parents. See the Student Budget Worksheet from the Government of Canada: www.canada.ca/en/financial-consumer-agency/services/budget-student-life/student-budget-worksheet.html	☐	
Get in the best physical condition and mentally prepare to play at the next level. You are a university/junior player now. You cannot train and prepare yourself like a high school player. Get the off-season strength and conditioning program from your new team.	☐	
Continue developing your positional skills a *minimum* of three times per week. Becoming a student of the game will help you achieve long-term success in your post-secondary career.	☐	
Time management will be critical. Develop a daily routine, as it will help you be more organized and efficient with your time.	☐	

If possible, plan to go back to the university campus for an orientation to familiarize yourself with the campus. Know the locations of the bookstore, lecture halls, physio centre, weight room, and cafeteria. If you're playing junior, go to the practice facilities and surrounding areas to become familiar with them.	☐
Where are you going to live—on or off campus? Do you plan to have a roommate or live on your own?	☐
If you are moving away from home, make sure your living arrangements are in place well before training camp starts.	☐
Where and how will you eat? For example, will you purchase a meal plan on campus, or do you plan to go grocery shopping?	☐
Find out from your new coaches if you can have access to playbooks and film to study. Getting a head start on the playbook is beneficial. You can't play fast and with confidence if your playbook knowledge is lacking.	☐
The goal is to earn playing time as soon as possible. It would be beneficial to study your team roster and the players who play your position again. *Know who you're competing against.*	☐
Talk to your coaches to specifically outline ways that you can earn playing time to help your team win games.	☐
Additional notes:	

COACH BURRIS INSIGHT:

At the university, junior, and CEGEP levels, coaches hold players accountable, and the expectation is that the players must rise to the team's standards. It's very important that you understand the coaches' expectations.

ENTERING YOUR FIRST YEAR OF UNIVERSITY

Coming out of high school and going to university will be the most difficult year of your career because you're in a transitional phase. Your high school routine is now gone. In university, you will develop a new routine and adjust to how things work as a student athlete. After year one of university, you typically find your groove and have time to develop your time-management skills.

> *I wish I knew how many hours a day is spent on football. It's not just "go to practice and go home." We have a lot of meetings and there is a lot of watching film, I am learning that there is a lot more elements to watching film.*

> Cam Michaud, defensive line
> University of Guelph Gryphons

"THE BEST PLAYER PLAYS"

It's important to know what you're getting into when you begin playing university-, junior-, or CEGEP-level football. When I began playing CEGEP football after high school, I was in for a rude awakening, as I thought everyone would get the opportunity to play. I was wrong. The competition level elevated, and players were competing at every practice. They had the mindset that the "best players played," and that's why practices were so intense—everyone was out to prove they were the best so they could dress and play on game day. If you understand this rule, you will embrace competition and be mentally prepared. No matter what level you play post-high school, you will encounter "the best player plays."

POTENTIAL POSITION CHANGE AT THE NEXT LEVEL

The reality is that players entering university or junior football go through position changes, both wanted and unwanted. For example, you may have been a wide receiver when you played high school football, and when you get to the next level, your coaches want you to play defensive back. Now you have to learn a new position and start from ground zero, which can be a fun challenge or unexpected and overwhelming.

WHY DO COACHES CHANGE PLAYERS' POSITIONS?

- Coaches want to put players in the best position to help the team win.
- The coaching staff notices that you have a better skill set in another position.
- They might have too many players at one position, and changing would be the best opportunity for you to receive playing time.

The best way to handle position changes is to trust that your coach is making the correct decision, believe in yourself, accept the challenge, buy into your new role, and work hard to be the best at that position.

BE PANDEMIC-PROOF

We have never seen a pandemic hit the world and turn our lives upside down the way COVID-19 has. The world has made major adjustments in efforts to get back to normal. The sun keeps rising and the day keeps going. If you are or were a high school senior who's gone through the recruiting process, then you know it has been challenging not having a season to gain exposure and consistent training, and not being able to go on campus visits. Making a decision about which university program to attend without a campus visit is very difficult. On the positive side, you can still get coaches at the post-secondary level to evaluate and recruit you. Here are a few tips:

- Post and share videos of yourself weight training. For example, coaches want to see videos of a high school lineman hang-cleaning or power-cleaning 315 pounds, dunking a basketball on a 10-foot rim, jumping a crazy vertical of 40-plus inches, or running an elite 40-time special. These videos will catch the coaches' attention.
- You can send coaches football-specific drills, such as bag drills, cone and ladder drills, and any position-specific skill work, which will help you get evaluated.
- Continue to build relationships with coaches by sending your latest highlight tapes.
- Be sure to be available for requested video meetings from coaches. You can also request to talk to coaches, as this would be one of the best ways for them to get to know you in person.
- University teams host open recruiting meetings through online video conference calls. This is where players and parents can learn more about the university and its football program. These meetings are valuable and it is strongly suggested to attend. Talk to your coaches to find out additional information about when teams have these recruiting meetings, or you can contact the football program of your choice to find out dates and times.

While in a pandemic, you can take the time to research and plan your next move post-high school graduation. Players can contact coaches via text, direct messages, emails, and phone calls. During a pandemic, do not expect unofficial or official campus visits, and coaches can't do home visits.

We have learned something from this pandemic at least: regardless of the restrictions, life continues, especially for football recruiting. Coaches will continue to look for players, so make sure not to get left behind. Take charge of your recruiting and stay proactive and pandemic-proof.

CHAPTER 10

Parents' Section

There is no worse feeling than not being able to help your child. As a coach, I have had many conversations with parents asking for help. In response, I ask them simple questions such as, "What position does your child play?" or, "Does your child have a highlight tape?" and the reply is something like, "I don't know," or a blank stare. Parents, the reality is you will need to do your own research regarding recruiting and post-secondary education. You will need to understand the available pathways so you can support your child's goals. The questions and answers below will provide clarity to help parents and their children be successful as you navigate through the recruiting process.

Parents frequently ask the following questions:

What options are available for playing football after high school?

Below is a list of post-secondary football options:

- CJFL Canadian Junior Football League: cjfl.org

- U Sports Canadian University Football: usports.ca/en/sports/football/m

- CEGEP: translate.google.com/translate?hl=en&sl=fr&u=http://rseq.ca/sports/football/collegial/division-1/&prev=search&pto=aue

- NCAA Football in the United States: ncaa.com/sports/football/fbs

- NJCAA Junior College Football in the United States: njcaa.org/sports/fball/index

How long are players eligible? How does eligibility work for CJFL and U Sports?

CJFL Canadian Junior Football league players must be twenty-two or under to play. Athletes who turn twenty-three in the calendar year are unable to play.

For U Sports Canadian university football, student athletes have five years of athletic eligibility, unless they turn twenty-five before the five years expire.

Canadian university players are eligible for the Canadian Football League draft three years after completing their first year of eligibility.

COACH BURRIS INSIGHT:

If your child plays junior football and has plans of playing U Sports football, they can play two years of football before their U Sports eligibility clock starts ticking. So, if they play three years of junior football and transfer to U Sports, they will have four years of eligibility instead of five years.

How do university and junior recruiters find players?

Recruiters attend football tournaments, showcase events, and private and university camps. They attend local and provincial championship games and national football tournaments. They receive recommendations from high school coaches, and players or parents may contact football programs. Recruiters may attend your child's practice, and they search video and analytics platform and social media platforms to find potential players. Your player should fill out the team's online recruiting form.

Should players wait to be discovered, or should players contact coaches?

The number one rule is to *never* wait to be recruited! Contact as many junior and university football programs as possible to get the ball rolling. When reaching out to junior and university coaches, you specifically want to contact the head coach or the recruiting coordinator. The best way to contact the head coach or the recruiting coordinators is by visiting the team's website, going to the coach's roster, and looking for the coach's contact information.

Another option is to contact coaches through the team's social media page or the coach's personal social media page. Once you have found the coach's information, reach out. If your child plans to attend university, the coaches only require their academic transcripts and highlight film. From there, the coaches can evaluate your child's film and grades. If your child is a fit, the coach will contact them. If your child is looking to play junior football, they only need to provide their highlight tape and game film to the coaches. Be sure to have a tape prepared and academic transcripts available.

How can my child get noticed even though he does not play on an elite high school team?

Coaches want to see your child live and in person, so attending university camps to gain exposure, sending out game film, and trying out for the elite programs like provincial teams will help them increase their exposure level. If you follow the action plans in this book, your child's exposure level will increase.

Will my child face a disadvantage playing in a rural lower-tier level compared to the city athletes playing against better competition when it comes to provincial/elite tryouts? Do they need to stand out immediately?

No, there is not a disadvantage. All players have to come to tryouts and stand out right away. If a player from a rural area comes to the tryout and clearly demonstrates that they are of a higher talent level, they have a good chance of making the team. It comes down to the player's character and whether they can help the team win games. Coaches want to know if the athlete can compete against top-level talent and play at a high level. Where you live and the tier on which your team plays is irrelevant.

Should families pay a recruiting agent?

This is an important question, because some families believe they are paying a fee with a guarantee that the agent will find a team. It would not be appropriate to tell a family where to spend their hard-earned money. However, other options exist to help your child develop into a complete student athlete. Recruiting agents and agencies are simply middlemen. They can provide knowledge and insight about how the recruiting process works in Canada and the United States. Families pay the recruiting agent to use their network of coaches to hopefully find a program for their client. However, keep in mind that recruiting agents have little influence on whether a team will recruit or sign an athlete. The final decision regarding which players will be signed comes from the head coach, recruiting coordinator, and staff. Do your research if you are considering using a recruiting agent's services, as the recruiting agency process can be done on your own.

What is the difference between CJFL and university ball?

In the CJFL, players are not required to be enrolled in school. University football players must be enrolled in school and are required to maintain a specific grade-point average to play football each year. Junior football allows the players to develop their positional and football skills and intelligence, and mature both physically and mentally without worrying about the expense or stress of university classes.

The majority of players who play junior football, if they go straight to playing university football, would be on the *scout team*. The scout team players practice daily to develop their overall skills. Additionally, they assist the *dress team* players to prepare for weekly games. Players become well-rounded by competing at the junior level, as they are exposed to more practices and games and receive one-on-one coaching, allowing them to develop into solid football players.

University education is independent learning, and student athletes are expected to keep up academically. Playing football at the university level is more about preparing the team to win the next game. Player development will happen more during the off season at the university level, but game planning and scheming, and preparing the players for the next game, are the priorities.

In junior football, there is not much of a structured off-season training program. Some teams run spring camps, and some may send out online workout plans to their players to train independently.

COACH BURRIS INSIGHT:

Some teams will have non-contact practices during the winter at an indoor facility.

University teams have mandatory weight-room sessions during the football season. Normally, the dress players will work out twice per week, and the non-dress players will work out three to four times per week. The redshirt and non-dress players have more scheduled workouts because it's a part of the development process, and generally they have a bigger gap to close in the weight room than the dress players. University football teams have mandatory team strength and conditioning workouts four to five times per week in the second semester. Failing to attend winter workouts could result in dismissal from the team. University off-season training is also intense and competitive, and coaches want their players to gain results. Off-session training includes team-building sessions, competition drills, and mental challenges where players are asked to think while fatigued.

Everyone is talented on university football teams. This is why the level of competition increases. You must be ready and willing to compete and earn your spot on the team. One of the head coach's duties is to build a winning program, so players must maintain focus and minimize mistakes. The coach's job is to recruit to build a solid football program and create competition within the team.

At the university level, the coaching staff will also have a small role in players' academics. Coaches and/or the team academic advisors can be found in the study hall, helping players with their schoolwork. As needed, programs will bring in tutors to help the players study. But, as mentioned previously, university is independent learning, so your student athlete will have to do the majority of their studying and make sure they are completing assignments and preparing for exams on their own.

Coaches or the team academic advisor will also assist with setting up academic plans and class selection so players can have the best shot at being successful. They will also have access to players' grades to make sure they're staying on track.

Can players go to multiple tryouts?

Yes. At the junior and university level, there are no limitations to how many tryouts a player can attend.

Should players tell teams they have committed to another program?

Yes. Players should inform teams who are recruiting them that they have committed to another program. In junior football team tryouts are in the spring, and first-year players and returning players must commit to their respective teams by signing a letter of intent on the official signing day, which is June 1.

Are all tryouts pay-to-play events?

It all depends on the football program and how its spring camp is run. Some programs will have fees associated with tryouts/spring camp, and some will not. Be prepared to pay a tryout fee, plus meals and accommodations.

Are the tryouts a typical combine form, or is there more to it?

On the first day, there might be a typical combine format. The rest of the tryouts will consist of multiple practices, and most teams end with a scrimmage to put everything together. There will be film with position coaches, and installations of plays. Every program is different, and tryouts and spring camps might be organized differently.

How long after a tryout before players find out if they made the team?

At the university and junior football level, players will know on the last day of spring camp, or they will be contacted the week following.

When will recruiters start looking for players and talking to them?

Canadian university football programs work a year or two ahead when recruiting. They start identifying players in Grade 10. In Grade 11, they will begin contacting players to start the recruiting process. Trying to get recruited in Grade 12 may be too late.

What do each of these terms mean?

- **Signed verbal commitment:** A player verbally agrees with the coach that he will be playing for their football program before signing the letter of intent.
- **Letter of intent:** A document with details that outline terms and conditions specific to that football program. In order to fully commit to a program, players must sign the letter of intent.
- **Signed:** The player has signed the letter of intent and is now fully committed to the team.

What does signing a letter of intent mean?

The recruit has signed a contract and committed to play football for that specific football program. Follow this link for additional information: usports.ca/uploads/hq/Forms/2017-18/ LOI_-_FAQ_and_interpretations.pdf or try searching for "letter of intent frequently asked questions."

Should players sign intent letters right away?

No. They should take the time to visit each program and/or attend each junior team of interest's spring camp. This gives the player an opportunity to get a feel for which program is the best fit. Once they are sure, they should sign the letter of intent.

Note: If your child is playing junior football, they cannot sign the letter of intent until June 1. At the U Sports level, there is not an official signing day for new players. Players attending university programs can sign anytime except during recruiting blackout periods. So, you can potentially sign as early as September 1 and as late as the following summer.

Is the player then obligated to play there?

Yes, they are obligated to play for that team once they sign the letter of intent. You can request a release at the junior level, although it can be difficult to get your release from that specific junior team. At the university level, you can decommit to the university program.

If a player signs to a team, can they go to other tryouts?

No. Once a player has signed the letter of intent, he is committed to playing for that team.

What does it mean when a player makes the team? Will they dress for games?

When the athlete makes the team at the junior and university level, he will practice and do all the team activities during on- and off-seasons. Just because your child is on the team does *not* mean they will dress for games. Teams have a specific number of players they are allowed to dress for games. Players must compete in practice each week and demonstrate to the coaches they know the playbook and the game plan to be selected to dress for games.

When are players confirmed to the roster?

Junior teams must submit their team roster of sixty-five players on September 15. If a player is not on the list, he can still practice with the team but cannot play games. The sixty-five-player roster cannot be changed after September 15.

What does it mean to redshirt?

At the university level, players who redshirt will only practice for the season and not dress for games. This allows the player to develop his football skills and athletics, and/or enable him to focus on school if he is struggling academically. The same rules apply at the junior level as the university level. Players will not dress for games but will focus on developing as a player.

Should players talk to coaches if they have more than one offer?

Offers happen mainly at the university level. Canadian universities offer Athletic Financial Awards, and athletic scholarships are offered in the United States. If you have not signed the letter of intent at a specific university football program, feel free to explore all your options.

At the junior level, June 1 is the national signing day. Once you sign the letter of intent, all communication with other coaches must stop.

Junior programs do not typically offer players financial support, as at the university level. All teams operate differently. Depending on the junior team's budget, they might have limited educational awards set up for players who are in school. These details can be clarified when speaking with the coaches.

What types of fees are associated with post-secondary teams? CJFL? Canadian university? American ball?

Junior football fees include:

- team registration
- team clothing packs
- living-away-from-home costs: rent, food, personal care items, and transportation expenses.
- football equipment and accessories (cleats, gloves, socks, etc.)

Canadian university fees include:

- tuition
- student fees
- books
- school supplies and equipment
- team clothing packs
- football equipment and accessories (cleats, gloves, socks, etc.)
- living-away-from-home costs: rent, food, personal care items, transportation expenses, and spending money
- football equipment and accessories

NCAA DI athletic scholarship fees include:

- personal care items, clothing, and spending money
- tuition, meals, housing, school supplies, and course textbooks are all covered

What types of supports do teams typically offer—team/position training, social events, meetings, etc.?

Depending on the program, whether it be junior or university football, these are some of the supports that could be offered:

- structured strength and condition training
- injury and recovery treatments

- free academic support, like tutoring and study hall
- assistance seeking employment and post-football career guidance
- volunteer and community involvement opportunities
- team-building events

What benefits can CJFL recruiters offer fairly? Housing? Scholarships?

There are no limitations on what CJFL teams can offer a player. It depends on the team's scholarship budget. Not every player is offered a scholarship or financial support, so be sure to have that conversation with the head coach and ensure that any financial arrangements are included in the letter of intent upon signing.

What benefits can universities fairly offer?

University football programs can only cover academic classes. Across Canada, each team can only offer a limited number of Athletic Financial Awards, and each athletic conference has unique details related to how a player is eligible. To receive an Athletic Financial Award, students must maintain a specific grade-point average.

What is the U Sports Central Identification Number?

Student athletes who want to participate at the Canadian university level must register for a U Sports Central Identification Number. They will also need this prior to official campus visits during the recruiting process. The U Sports number allows U Sports Central to track student athletes' academics and monitor athletic information and eligibility. U Sports is responsible for enforcing recruiting guidelines.

Can CJFL players also go to school or work?

Yes, players can go to school or work. It depends on the player's goals.

What documents can players expect to sign for CJFL? University?

At the junior level, players will sign the letter of intent, CJFL and team registration forms, a waiver, and liability agreements. In university, players will sign the letter of intent, team registration forms, liability forms, admissions paperwork, player roster information, and medical forms. These forms are the most common, but there may be others.

Is there a difference between the CJFL and university season?

Yes, there is a big difference. In university you must attend daily classes, complete readings, assignments, and, if necessary, attend study hall. Players also need to complete a mandatory two to four in-season workouts per week, watch the team's films on their own and with their positional group and the team, and attend team meetings and practices. At the university level, receiving treatment when you are injured is also mandatory.

In junior, you have daily practices and weekly games. Attending school is not mandatory, so that allows for less structure during the day for the players. Being a student athlete in university provides academic structure. This is the real reason players attend university. Junior football is also more independent, as in-season workouts are not mandatory, and you're expected to lift on your own. The football skill and competition levels in practice and in games are higher at the university level.

What is the length of the regular season and training camp?

Junior football spring camp is three to four days. The pre-season followed by the season begins in the last week of July, and the national championship game is in November.

Note: Each conference may start earlier or later. University spring camp is three to five days. The main training camp begins in the middle of August, the season begins in September, and the national championship—the Vanier Cup—is in November.

Are players expected to relocate for just the season, or all year?

For university, unless you are going to a local institution, players will need to relocate during the academic year. The best practice for the student athlete is to be at school for the whole academic year. This allows him to focus on academics, strength and conditioning training, and bonding with teammates. If your child is playing junior football away from home and not tied down with school or work commitments, they can move back home after the football season.

Should students take a full course load when playing?

It depends on how well organized the student is and their time-management skills. Some players might take three to four courses the first semester during the season, then take a heavier course load in the second semester and summer school to stay on track to graduate.

Do both university and CJFL teams have health insurance for players?

All teams must have team insurance. It is mandatory.

Many players are minors. Will recruiters contact parents or just players?

Recruiters tend to contact the players first and then the parents. It also depends on whether parents have initiated contact with the recruiter.

Do American university football teams require students to write the SATs?

Yes. Visit the college board website for more details: collegeboard.org.

Should I attend university campus visits with my child?

Yes. If you can attend the campus visits, it will help you understand what the university has to offer, as well as allow you the opportunity to meet the coaches. Most importantly, it allows you to ask questions in person.

COACH BURRIS INSIGHT:

Have your list of questions to ask the coaches on campus prepared in advance. You and your child should leave the campus visit with a clear picture of what the university, football program, and coaches are like. In addition, you should know where your child will fit in at that program.

COACH BURRIS INSIGHT:

Some campus visits might be out of province, and the program will only pay for your child's travel and accommodations. You might not attend these visits, but you may still contact the coach prior to the visit to have any questions or concerns answered.

These are common questions that have been asked by parents and players. Hopefully the answers have given you some clarity. If you have additional questions that has gone unlisted, feel free to forward your questions to coachburris@ironwillfootball.ca and I would be happy to answer them.

What parents should avoid

At the post-secondary level, coaching staff put in numerous hours preparing a game plan to defeat the opponent. In addition, coaches always evaluate their own players' performance in the previous game and the week of practice leading up to the next game. You might be asking yourself, "Why so much player evaluation?" Coaches want to make sure they are putting the best players on the field in order to win games.

With all this being said, I want to give parents some advice. If for some reason your child is not receiving as much playing time as expected, no playing time at all, not dressing for games, or has been asked to change position, please, please, please do not allow the knee-jerk reaction of contacting the coaches for answers. We understand that you want to help your child, but doing that could do more harm than good for your child. Coaches get turned off when parents take the approach of attacking coaches to help their child.

The best course of action would be to encourage your child to speak to his position coach. If they get no answers, they should move up the chain of command and talk with the defensive or offensive coordinator, and then the head coach. If there are still no solutions offered, *this* would be the appropriate time for you to step in and talk to the head coach. Just be sure to allow your child to communicate with the coaches before you step in. As a former university and junior coach, I have witnessed this situation far too often. Simple communication goes a long way. Trust me on this advice—you'll thank me later!

CHAPTER 11

Conclusion

Now that you have reached the end of the book, you should feel more comfortable about the recruiting process and clearly understand what you need to do to be recruited, commit, and sign to the post-secondary football program that's best for you. Your recruiting success will come down to good academics if you want to play at the university level, performance on game day, and being proactive during your recruiting journey.

You and your family have put in the hard work and dedication to get to this point on the way to playing post-secondary football. Enjoy the experience and do not take playing football at the next level for granted. Not everyone makes it to the next level, but with the right attitude and effort, you can increase your chances of taking your football career to the next stage.

FOOTBALL TEMPLATES AND RESOURCES

INTRODUCTION LETTER TO UNIVERSITY/JUNIOR COACHES

Here is an example of a short but to-the-point letter to introduce yourself to post-secondary football programs. Remember, coaches have limited time, so make your letter concise and to the point and provide only information they need to know about you.

COACH BURRIS INSIGHT:

Be sure to have a subject heading that stands out so coaches open your email.

Hello Coach Grey:

My name is Jackson Fresh. I am 6 foot 5, 280 pounds, and I play defensive and offensive line at Cedarbrae Collegiate institution in Scarborough, Ontario. I am interested in attending the University of Moorelands because I am academically interested in business. The University of Moorelands has an excellent business program and a nationally ranked football program that I want to play for.

I will be graduating from high school in the spring of 2030. Currently, my academic grade-point average is at a 4.0.

I have attached my most recent academic transcripts, highlight tape, and my high school and community coaches' contact information just in case you need to contact them for additional details about me.

Any feedback on my highlight tape would be greatly appreciated. Is there a time when I can follow up with you regarding my interest in being a student athlete at the University of Moorelands?

I can be reached at 416-111-1111 or at JacksonF@ gmail.com.

Thank you for your time and consideration.

Jackson Fresh

FOOTBALL RÉSUMÉ EXAMPLE

Here is an example of a football résumé that will give coaches a better idea of who you are as a student athlete. You can send your résumé when you send your highlight tape and cover letter.

COACH BURRIS INSIGHT:

A football résumé is not mandatory, but it gives coaches a better scope of who you are.

Jackson Fresh

403-111-1111
J.Fresh@mail.com

PLAYER INFORMATION

High School	Cedarbrae Collegiate Institute
Birth Date	January 21, 2002
Height	6'5"
Weight	280 pounds
University Education Interest	Accounting or Human Resource Management
Grade-Point Average (GPA)	4.0
Position	Defensive linemen
Multi-Sport Athlete	Basketball, rugby, track and field

ATHLETIC INFORMATION

Cedarbrae Colts Football Team 2030 (High School)

- Alberta provincial champion
- Lineman of the game in the provincial championship
- Team linemen of the year

Team Alberta 2029 (Provincial Football)

- Won silver in the Canada Cup tournament
- Team captain of Team Alberta
- On the players leadership committee with Team Alberta

Cedarbrae Colts Football Team 2029 (High School)

- Played offensive line and defensive line
- District football champion
- Won team leadership award

Scarborough Thunder Varsity Football 2028 (Summer Football)

- Alberta Varsity Football League champions
- Played defensive line and offensive linemen

Coaches References

Coach Victory, Head Coach, Cedarbrae Colts Football
Direct: 403-333-3333, Ext. 2000; email: victory@cci.ca

Coach Smith, Head Coach, U18 Team Alberta
Direct: 403-444-4444; email: smith@teamalberta.ca

RESOURCES

Some resources to help in your research:

Organization	Website	Notes
NCAA	ncaa.com	The official website for the NCAA
NCAA	ncaa.org	This will be especially important for students looking to attend NCAA
NCAA	ncaa.org/student-athletes/future/canada	Academic requirements by province to play at the NCAA level
Eligibility Center	eligibilitycenter.org	Student athletes who would like to compete at the NCAA level *must* register with the Eligibility Center
U Sports	usports.ca	The official website for Canadian University Athletics
Maclean's	macleans.ca/hub/education-rankings/	Provides information on university rankings in Canada
Canadian Junior Football League	cjfl.org	The official website of the Canadian Junior Football League
CEGEP	cegepsquebec.ca/en/	College in Quebec
CEGEP	translate.google.com/translate?hl=en&sl=fr&u= http://rseq.ca/sports/football/collegial/division-1/&prev=search&pto=aue	RSEQ CEGEP football
CollegeTrackr	collegetrackr.com	CollegeTrackr educates Canadian students and athletes about educational opportunities in the United States.
U Sports Central	usportscentral.ca/studentcentre/	U Sports Central is where you register for your U Sports Identification number

Other helpful resources:

- High school guidance counsellors
- Post-secondary websites
- Post-secondary open house tours
- University academic calendars

THIRD-PARTY RECRUITING AGENCIES

Recruiting agencies *do not* have any influence or final say when football programs decide which athlete will receive an Athletic Financial Award offer in Canada or scholarship offers in the United States. They do have connections to coaches, and depending on the person or the agency, some will have more contacts than others.

They will make a player profile that includes athletic details and the player's most recent highlight tape and email these to universities and college coaches. Recruiting agencies will sometimes make calls on behalf of the player to university and college coaches with whom they are connected. Some recruiters might provide insight into what steps need to be taken to play at the next level, which is valuable.

However, you can do a lot of what the recruiting agencies do on your own—especially with this guidebook. This is a key point, so it is worth repeating: recruiting agencies have no influence on whether or not you receive an offer for a school at the university level. The key factors that determine whether you receive an offer are your grades and how you perform on the football field.

I have witnessed families shell out a lot of money to third-party agencies and get left with no results or signings. It would be more beneficial to direct your money to an academic tutor, strength and conditioning programs, camps, or positional skill development instead of a recruiting agency.

GLOSSARY

Athletic Financial Award (AFA): Any award that is conditional to being listed on the official U Sports eligibility certificate and administered by the university's awards office consistent with the awarding university's policies.

Athletic scholarship: There are two types of athletic scholarships: full and partial, which are offered to players who play in the NCAA and compete at the DI or DII levels in the United States. An athletic scholarship is financial aid offered to the student athlete by the university or college athletic department.

CEGEP: A college that offers a two-year pre-university program that is mandatory for Quebec students who want to attend university. Out-of-province students attend CEGEP to upgrade their academics to be accepted into university.

COACH BURRIS INSIGHT:

There are also English-speaking CEGEPs in Quebec.

Combines: Events or clinics where players perform various football-specific drills and exercises to rate and rank their overall athletic ability and football potential.

Decommit: When a player verbally commits to one football program without signing the letter of intent and later decides to withdraw from the initial program to commit to another.

Eyeball test: When post-secondary coaches meet you in person or visit you at your high school or a football game. They will be looking at your physical stature to see if you're really the height and weight listed. Understand that some teams take the eyeball test seriously and want their players to be at a specific height and weight, while other programs just care if players can make plays on the football field.

COACH BURRIS INSIGHT:

Be honest when listing your height, weight, and any athletic information.

Grade-Point Average (GPA): A numbered scale between 1.0 to 4.0 that shows how well your grades are in your academic classes.

Highlight tape: A collection of video clips that showcase the player's talent. They are sent out by the player to university and college football programs for evaluation. The benefit of a highlight tape is that it allows coaches to evaluate the player and decide if he fits their program. If the player fits the football program, then coaches will proceed to the next phase of the recruiting process.

Hudl: A popular platform football teams use across the country to store practice and game film. Coaches and players can also communicate and prepare for games with it. You can review games, practices, and make correction notes. Hudl also has a feature where players can create their highlight tapes with clips from the past season.

I-20: International students will need to apply for the I-20 visa if they go to school in the United States. The I-20 document can only be issued by schools that are certified by the US Department of Homeland Security. For more details, see the "Study in the States" page on the Department of Homeland Security website: studyinthestates.dhs.gov/students/prepare/students-and-the-form-i-20

Canadian Junior Football League (CJFL): A competitive league that reaches from Ontario to British Columbia. Players twenty-two years old and under can compete in the CJFL.

Letter of intent: A commitment between a prospective student athlete and a U Sports institution for the prospect of the player being a part of that institution's U Sports inter-university athletic program for the coming academic year.

National Association of Intercollegiate Athletics (NAIA): A college athletics association for small colleges and universities geographically ranging from British Columbia to one in the US Virgin Islands and the rest in the United States.

National Collegiate Athletic Association (NCAA): An organization that supervises and regulates student athletes, competition divisions, conferences, and institutions.

NCAA Eligibility Center: The first step of the recruiting process, and where your academic transcript records and SAT scores are reviewed. This is an important step to playing in the NCAA and receiving a DI or DII level scholarship. The NCAA Eligibility Center manages the student athlete's eligibility status.

National Junior College Athletic Association (NJCAA): This league is played throughout the United States. Community colleges, state colleges, and junior colleges are associated with the NJCAA. *JUCO* is a short term meaning "junior college." JUCO football is only played in the United States.

Offer (scholarship or Athletic Financial Award): An offer is a scholarship (NCAA) or an AFA (U Sports) designed to assist student athletes in paying for their university undergraduate degree.

Official off-campus visit: When a prospective student athlete meets with an institution representative for a meal or meeting exclusively outside of the boundaries of the university campus or buildings controlled by the athletic department. An institution may fund, in whole or in part, a prospective student athlete's official off-campus visit once every 365 days, to a maximum of two official off-campus visits in the prospective student athlete's lifetime (see unofficial off-campus visit below).

Official on-campus visit: When a prospective student athlete is invited to an institution and receives financial assistance for the visit by an institutional representative. An institution may fund, in whole or in part, a prospective student athlete's visit once every 365 days to a maximum of two visits in the prospective student athlete's lifetime. An official visit cannot exceed 72 hours from the time of arrival on campus until the time of departure from campus. Institutionally funded attendance at formal ID camps, evaluation camps, and/or individual evaluation sessions organized by an institution is considered to be an official on-campus visit (see unofficial on-campus visit below).

Recruit: Someone being pursued by university and college coaches. University and college coaches will stay in contact and engage with the recruit in efforts to commit them to their football program.

Recruiting: The solicitation of a prospective student athlete, or a prospective student athlete's parents, legal guardian, relatives, or coach(es), by an institution's representative for the purpose of securing the student athlete's enrollment and ultimate participation in the institution's U Sports athletic program.

Recruiting blackout: The Canadian recruiting blackout periods are restricted to football during the following times: December 23 to January 2, within five days of the start of the CIS East-West All-Star Game and until one clear day following the completion of the game, and the month of July with the exemption of the Canada Cup national tournament, where only players participating at the tournament can be recruited.

Redshirt: A athlete who has withdrawn from university competition for a year to develop his football skills or improve his academic grades. Players who redshirt extend their playing eligibility by one year.

Standardized College Admissions Test (SAT): Required for student athletes who compete in the NCAA. Refer to page 20 in the NCAA Football section for SAT updates

Signed: When a player has signed the letter of intent and has committed to attend that specific university and play football for their program.

Unofficial off-campus visit: When an institution's representative watches a prospective student athlete practice and/or compete for the purpose of evaluation, or engages in conversation with them outside of the physical boundaries of the university campus or buildings controlled by the athletic department without providing financial assistance.

Unofficial on-campus visit: When a prospective student athlete meets institution representatives where some or all of the visit occurs within the physical boundaries of the university campus or buildings controlled by the athletic department, but receives no financial assistance of any kind.

U Sports: The Canadian national governing body of university sports.

U Sports eligibility: Players are eligible to play varsity football for five years. The student athlete (football player) must use their five years of eligibility within a seven-year period from high school graduation. In U Sports football, a student athlete eligibility clock starts ticking at age twenty.

U Sports identification number: U Sports has made an official registry database to collect and track recruits and current players competing at the U Sports level and to better understand their athletes. It is mandatory for every student athlete attending a Canadian university to register and have a U Sports identification number.

U Sports letter of intent: A commitment between a prospective student athlete and a U Sports institution with respect to the prospect of being a part of that institution's U Sports inter-university athletic program for the coming academic year.

Verbal commitment A student athlete will give a verbal commitment to the specific university prior to signing the letter of intent. This is a non-binding agreement a coach or student athlete can abolish at any time. Verbal commitments more commonly happen to players who are entering the NCAA.

Signing the letter of intent: Once a letter of intent is signed, a prospective student athlete is no longer subject to further recruiting contacts and calls. This will satisfy the objective of reducing recruiting pressure on student athletes. When the terms of an AFA are included, student athletes have written confirmation of those terms. Although a letter does not guarantee playing time or the presence of a particular coach, it facilitates a clear understanding of the terms of an AFA and can serve as a valuable tool in resolving any disputes that might arise. usports.ca/uploads/hq/Forms/2017-18/ LOI_-_FAQ_and_interpretations.pdf

REFERENCES

Canadian Junior Football League   Canadian Junior Football League Rules & Regulations PDF: cdn3.sportngin.com/attachments/document/0068/6004/CJFL_Rules_Regs_April_2014.pdf#_ga=2.131704527.1369690235.1610306015-135714948.1556863472

NCAA   Scholarship Limits 2020–21: scholarshipstats.com/ncaalimits

NCSA: ncsasports.org/football/division-1-collegesncsasports.org/recruiting

Times Higher Education World University Ranking: timeshighereducation.com/world-university-rankings/2021/world-ranking#!/page/3/length/25/sort_by/rank/sort_order/asc/cols/statsncaa.org/student-athletes/future/recruitingn csasports.org/ncaa-eligibility-center/recruiting-rules

U Sports   U Sports Central User Guide PDF: usports.ca/uploads/cis/About/athlete_info/2018-19/U_SPORTS_Central_User_Guide_%2818-19%29.pdf

usports.ca/uploads/hq/By_Laws-Policies-Procedures/2019/EN/Policy_40.10.1_to_40.10.6_Eligibility_Rules_%282019-2020%29.pdf

— **U Sports blackout dates**   U Sport Policies and Procedures 40.10.7 Recruiting Regulations PDF: usportscentral.ca/StudentCentre/Documents/Policy_40.10.7_EN.pdf

ABOUT THE AUTHOR

Coach Burris is a former U Sports student athlete and a Vanier Cup Champion. He has coached at the U Sports level and has over a decade of coaching experience ranging from bantam level to the university level. Coach Burris has worked with more than a thousand players across Canada. He also had the honor of coaching on the Alberta U18 Team for three years, in addition to running his football performance camps and defensive line academy program.

Manufactured by Amazon.ca
Bolton, ON